Recovery at Work

Recovery at Work

Using Twelve Step Principles for Professional Success

Amy Newman

BEP

BUSINESS EXPERT PRESS

Leader in applied, concise business books

First published in 2024 by
Business Expert Press, LLC
222 East 46th Street, New York, NY 10017
www.businessexpertpress.com

ISBN-13: 978-1-63742-740-8 (paperback)
ISBN-13: 978-1-63742-741-5 (e-book)

Business Expert Press Business Career Development Collection

First edition: 2024

10 9 8 7 6 5 4 3 2 1

Description

The tools I learned in recovery from addiction can help *anyone* find peace and develop resilience at work.

The principles behind Twelve Step programs such as Alcoholics Anonymous are simple but profoundly useful for restoring balance and building confidence. *Recovery at Work* provides practical examples for applying tools to overcome the stress and burnout of daily work life and to build a better career. Twelve Step principles have helped millions of people in recovery, and they can work for anyone.

Dozens of real, personal stories illustrate ways to handle work challenges and conflicts with honesty, humility, hope, compassion, and courage. Examples show how to find your footing—as though you're walking along a narrow ridge—without overreacting or numbing out.

With practice, you'll get better at discerning what you can and can't control at work. You'll learn to accept what you can't control and become more skillful at changing what you can control.

Contents

Preface

Having struggled with various addictions for much of my life, I needed a better solution for managing through life's challenges, including challenges at work. Vaguely aware of Twelve Step programs founded by Alcoholics Anonymous (AA) and used in more than a dozen recovery programs, I thought these groups were too religious for me. I also didn't think my case was serious enough for a meeting, but eventually, I went.

I learned that people of all or no religion are welcome, and I was excited about the focus on character. For years, I had been teaching and writing about character not as a tool for recovery but as a tool for communication and leadership. Principles explored in this book are from ancient Greek philosophers and are independent of AA, yet the Twelve Steps offer a structure for practicing them in our lives.

AA World Services, Inc., requests that authors avoid mentioning their Twelve Step program affiliation, and I have honored that tradition. Although some authors in recovery also use a pseudonym or their first name and last initial, I decided to use my real name. For me, avoiding my real name contradicts what I encourage students to do: to be their authentic, vulnerable, integral selves. I cannot write about addiction and fail to admit my own struggles.

I have also written the steps as AA World Services, Inc., requested: with "God" and with "Him" and "His" capitalized pronouns. My hope is that you can see this language as I see it, a tradition of AA I accept because it is beyond my control—a fundamental program lesson.

I write as an emeritus business communication faculty member, as a former human resources (HR) professional, and as a person in recovery. Of course, I don't speak for everyone; you might have suffered far more than I have in addiction, you might have other challenges, or you might simply have a tough time navigating the workplace, as many of us do. I use "we" because this book is for all of us who want to advance our career by improving how we work and how we interact with others. You may have experienced a Twelve Step program or are curious about them.

At times, I address "you" as an invitation to consider ideas in the book. Suggestions are based on my own and others' experience or on research, which is imperfect and evolving. Suggestions are for you to consider depending on your own situation. That's my disclaimer to say that the publisher and I are not liable for the results.

All stories in the book are based on real situations; some are compilations or extrapolations of stories. Names and other identifying information have been changed.

I am enormously grateful to my fellow travelers in recovery, including my sponsor, Kim B., for showing me a different way of life. My lifelong friend Jean U. suggested that I try the Twelve Step program that gave me a recovery community, and I'll never forget that. Several program friends have shaped my thinking, offered stories, and listened to my worries, particularly Kim B., Jean T., Rebecca G., and Joe M., who also encouraged me to write about the principles in the workplace and served as a reviewer. I'm grateful to Business Expert Press for the enthusiastic interest in publishing this book. Scott Isenberg has been a great source of ready, sensible guidance.

Two authors greatly shaped my thinking about recovery: Stephanie S. Covington (*A Woman's Way through the Twelve Steps*) and Kevin Griffin (*One Breath at a Time: Buddhism and the Twelve Steps*). In addition, their generosity in sharing their own writing and publishing experiences illustrates the core concept of service in Twelve Step programs.

I am most grateful to my partner, Eric Clay, who nudged me into recovery and encouraged me to deepen my writing and teaching over the years. He and my friend and colleague, Christy McDowell, have been the best writing partners and reviewers I could have asked for, engaging me on hundreds of questions about what the principles mean and how they can be practiced in the workplace. Christy introduced me to the writings of Martin Buber, whose concept of the narrow ridge is central to the book.

Despite my own time in recovery and research for this book, I believe I know less now than when I started writing. As is usually the case with personal development, the closer we look, the more there is to see. I also recognize that writing with my full name increases my accountability to my sobriety and to my recovery. I'm grateful for that reality and accept the challenge.

Testimonials

"With thoughtfulness and creativity, Amy Newman has successfully applied the Twelve Steps recovery tools to the world of work. She identifies each Step's guiding principle and how it looks in behavior. She also offers guidance on achieving balance and judgment in the work environment, using real-life examples to highlight possibilities and pitfalls. Using these principles for living can make a significant contribution to the workplace and one's own well-being. It is a 'must-read' for everyone who is working."—**Stephanie S. Covington, PhD, LCSW; Author, *A Woman's Way through the Twelve Steps***

"I wish there was a book like this when I was working. The procedures addressed in Recovery at Work would have helped me in my interactions with direct reports. Amy provides tools to establish a consistent and positive solution to problems faced in the workplace. Using the principles in the book would have greatly assisted me in handling an area that I found difficult to address. Simplifying the approach to problems that many people find complicated is one of Amy's many talents."—**John Svensson, Retired Hospitality Executive; Former Director of Catering with Hyatt Corporation, Starwood Hotels, and Statler Hotel at Cornell University**

"I, like so many others, struggle to find balance in my professional life and was helped by Amy Newman's fresh perspective of the 'narrow ridge' for applying Twelve Step principles in an accessible way.

I highly recommend Recovery at Work for anyone seeking coping tools for managing stress, triggers, or toxicity in their professional life.

I work with many who seek recovery and will be putting this engaging guide for finding balance at work in their hands."—**Beth Fisher Sanders, LCSW, LCAS; Psychotherapist, recovery advocate, and person in long-term recovery; Alternatives – CEO, HOPE Recovery Resources; President Emeritus, NARR (National Alliance for Recovery Residences)**

"A 'must-read' for business professionals striving for work-life balance in our highly stressful post-COVID workplace. Using multiple examples drawn from her experience in management, in the classroom, and in recovery, Amy Newman invites us to develop coping strategies for feeling competent and productive at work and for building satisfying relationships. Share this book with your friends and colleagues."—**Janis Forman, PhD, Professor Emerita of Management, UCLA Anderson School of Management**

"Recovery at Work *is a candid, insightful, and practical walk through real issues facing real people. Professor Newman masterfully shares insights from her own experience and the experiences of dozens of others, grounded in the science of recovery. In a moment when supporting mental health is a top priority for most major employers, the book offers a unique lens on an incredibly important and timely topic."*—**Josh, Human Resources Executive**

Introduction

The "Narrow Ridge" Is a Guide

Work can be a toxic place, leading to stress, burnout, addiction, or relapse. Whether you're in recovery from an addiction, trying to get sober, facing other challenges, feeling as though work is threatening your mental health, or simply having difficulty navigating the workplace, this book is for you.

I wrote this book because I wish I had such a resource earlier in my career, when I was struggling with various addictions. At the time, I had limited emotional awareness and few tools to manage through the daily challenges at work. Looking forward to "unwinding" after work (and eventually, indulging too much of the time) was my best solution to feel at peace.

Since then, I found better solutions that are available to anyone. This book offers a window into the tools people use to get and stay sober—and shows how they can be practiced at work to overcome any obstacles.

Some of us have extra challenges at work. We might be more sensitive; we feel our feelings more acutely and use substances or compulsive behaviors just to feel normal.[1] Our fears and character issues may come raging back during the stress of a job, including working with others who have their own struggles. If you have a spotty employment history or little experience managing in a professional environment, work may be even more difficult.

Work challenges can trigger self-centeredness, impulsive behavior, or anger. The structure and obligations of a job also may provoke the defiant nature some of us have in common. Some of us feel like outsiders, and we like it that way.

Every day at work also presents complex, ambiguous situations with no clear right-or-wrong answers. A common thinking problem, or cognitive distortion, of people with a history of addiction is all-or-nothing or black-and-white thinking.[2] In drinking (or other addictive substances or behaviors) and in thinking, moderation is not our strength.

My own struggle was complicated by my addiction to work. About four months into recovery, I realized I had made my employer my "higher power." Wherever I worked, I depended on the organization for guidance, for my self-esteem, and for a sense of community. Invariably, I would be disappointed. Whenever I got criticized at a job, my fears of rejection and abandonment would prevail, and I was convinced I would get fired. I had no balance and could turn my mind off only with other addictive behaviors and substances.

We need better strategies to replace old patterns of thinking and behaving—to avoid extremes and get comfortable in the gray areas. Philosopher and theologian Martin Buber described the "narrow ridge" surrounded by an abyss on each side.[3] You may feel as though you're constantly walking a treacherous path, teetering from side to side, trying to make good choices but struggling to find stable, middle ground. As we walk the narrow ridge, we develop coping strategies—to be *sober*, or steady, balanced, and sensible, without going to extremes despite the challenges we face.

Buber's early description of the narrow ridge is a place where we don't, at first, see the abysses. Only when we get to the end of the ridge do we notice the raging depths on either side, and only then are we afraid. Because the ridge is circular, this spot also marks the beginning, a chance for us to start anew.[4] To recover means "to regain consciousness," "regain health or strength," and to "return."[5] Maybe we return to who we used to be before we fell off course, or we regain strength after being in a workplace that saps our energy and damages our self-esteem.

Starting anew means facing our fears. Some of us drank, took pills, ate, shopped, gambled—anything to avoid our fears—which, at times, just inflated them. Sober, we no longer stagger blindly across the ridge. In recovery, we see the abysses clearly, but our fear propels us forward rather than derails us or stops us in our tracks.

We Practice Recovery Tools at Work

For all its stress, work can be a healing place. Learning new things, achieving goals, working with others, and of course, making money help us feel competent and productive. Through work, we're contributing members of society and find connection, which we hear at recovery meetings is the "opposite of addiction."

Work is also a great place to practice recovery tools. Where else can you get a screaming customer, broken equipment, conflict with a coworker, flaming email, and last-minute budget request all in one day? Thorny work situations that would have stymied us in the past are now opportunities to hone our skills and develop new habits. With practice, we "intuitively know how to handle situations which used to baffle us."[6]

Let's say you start a new business. At once, you worry about failure and success, about not getting any sales and about getting so many orders you can't fill them. At once, you're conflicted about a recent hire: happy with their ideas but frustrated by their lack of follow through. These are natural, paradoxical concerns.

Buber described the narrow ridge as a place between alternatives and invites us to hold two oppositions simultaneously.[7] Those of us with addiction histories know this paradoxical place. We're never really "recovered"; we're *in recovery*—both sober and still addicted. That's a quality of our lives: no longer either/or, but both and still more. In difficult work situations, one person isn't right and the other wrong. We consider both ourselves and others and affirm both. We work through what seem like contradictions, conflicts, and complexities and learn to act more skillfully.[8]

Here's Margaret's dilemma. One of dozens of real stories we explore in the book, this is a dramatic example with serious consequences. When in active addiction, Margaret didn't have the tools to manage through this decision:

When I was teaching at a residential program for at-risk boys, I saw Sarah, another teacher, who acted inappropriately with the students. She would let the boys play with her hair, and they watched movies together during breaks. Once I saw her talking to a 16-year-old outside his dorm. They talked for about two hours, and he didn't have a shirt on!

The kicker was when she told me she was planning to go to a town where I know that boy lived. I should have reported her, but I was on thin ice myself. I was drinking and using during the days and was the scapegoat—always getting in trouble for things I didn't do. The next day, I left and checked myself into a treatment facility.

When we went back to school in August, Sarah was gone. Someone said the boy's father caught them together on the couch in their home.

At the time, Margaret was too worried about her own standing to report the teacher. She also had good reasons for staying quiet: The behavior was public, so she wasn't the only one who saw it, and Margaret had reported issues in the past, and nothing was done. Now that Margaret has been in recovery, she sees that she had other choices and could have handled the situation differently. In others' stories throughout the book, you may see your own experiences, and you may identify with decisions made or ones that you would like to make.

We "Practice These Principles" and Strengthen Our Character

In this book, we practice principles from Twelve Step programs founded by Alcoholics Anonymous (AA) as tools to navigate the narrow ridge at work. The Twelve Step programs, used by more than a dozen recovery groups, aren't for everyone, and plenty of alternatives help people get and stay sober. I resisted a Twelve Step program but found that people of all religions, including nonreligious types like me, can benefit. The program offers a community and a process for recovery but isn't dogmatic.

Our focus in this book is not on the steps themselves but on the principles behind the steps. If you have experience with a Twelve Step program, you'll get a deeper dive into the principles—and a deeper approach to your recovery in the workplace. If this is your introduction to Twelve Step programs, you'll see how they have helped millions of people not only get and stay sober but live more peaceful, productive lives.

In the last step of any Twelve Step program, we're asked to "practice these principles in all our affairs."*[9] The principles are observable skills we can develop through practice. Not unique to Twelve Step programs, the principles are character strengths and virtues dating back to ancient Greek philosophers and are the foundation of the positive psychology field.[10]

In recovery, we strive to rid ourselves of character "defects," as they're called in Twelve Step programs (or defaults, defenses, or patterns). I call them weaknesses because we replace them with character strengths and virtues, which are the program principles.[11] Humility replaces arrogance, and compassion replaces apathy. Margaret's situation might demonstrate cowardice, which would be replaced by courage.

Character is the whole of who we are—how we live in the world and relate to others in every aspect of our lives. When we practice the principles, we demonstrate strong character. Here are a few workplace examples that illustrate the principles:

- You take responsibility for a mistake instead of blaming others. (Accountability)
- You point out a contract error that was in your favor. (Honesty)
- You stay late to help a direct report meet a deadline. (Service)
- You support an idea that you initially resisted. (Faith)
- You check that a customer isn't charged more than an advertised price. (Integrity)

In organizations, recruiting and performance evaluations don't focus enough on these principles (or character or virtues). We hire and promote for skills, knowledge, and abilities needed to perform a job, but strong character is what makes strong leaders.[12] Practicing the principles instead of succumbing to our fears is hard work. Having done the work, a person in recovery may be a better employee—someone an employer wants to hire.

---

* I want to acknowledge that an AA cofounder described the steps themselves as "a group of principles, spiritual in nature." But more recently, Twelve Step programs distinguish steps and associated principles.

The principles seem like common sense and, intellectually, they are. But we practice them every day until they become a natural part of who we are and how we live our lives, including our work life. In this book, you'll learn tangible ways you can use program principles as new tools to deepen your recovery and build confidence when faced with complex situations at work.

We Find Balance

Like our own black-and-white thinking in active addition, our culture tends toward dichotomies. We may think of character strengths or weaknesses—we're humble or arrogant, hopeful or depressed. But it's more helpful to think of being more or less skillful in how we practice principles throughout our career. We might find it easy to be compassionate with some coworkers but not others, or we might feel generous in the afternoon but not first thing in the morning.

We could use *too much* or *too little* of a character dimension or principle. If a character weakness is a *deficiency*, meaning using too little of a principle, then an *excess* is using too much of the principle.[13] Both can be harmful to ourselves and to others. For example, too little perseverance could be laziness, but too much perseverance could be perfectionism, which also causes harm.

Without an understanding of the extremes, we have a difficult time setting boundaries, another common problem discussed in recovery circles.[14] Boundaries are about setting limits—carving out physical, emotional, or thought space so we can maintain our well-being. As you'll read in each chapter, sometimes, too much of a principle—or being too *principled*—leads to losing a sense of ourselves, which is not healthy. This is the flip side of using too little of a principle, which also could lead to a loss of our grounded self. And yet, while boundaries are firm, they can shift as relationships change and we reassess our capabilities. We need to be both muscular and flexible as we walk along the narrow ridge to keep our balance.

The following table shows the AA steps as originally written and corresponding deficiencies and excesses. These steps, which draw on other movements, were published in *Alcoholics Anonymous*, the "Big Book," in the 1930s.[15] Since then, Twelve Step programs have expanded to other groups, some of which have updated the language to remove the gendered pronouns. In addition, the blanks in Step 1 and Step 12 are replaced with each group's focus, for example, alcohol/alcoholics, heroin/heroin addicts, food/compulsive overeaters, gambling/compulsive gamblers, social media/social media addicts, work/workaholics, or debt/compulsive debtors. In addition to the principles I've chosen,[†] I identify possible extremes of each.

STEP	DEFICIENCY (too little)	PRINCIPLE	EXCESS (too much)
1. We admitted we were powerless over _____—that our lives had become unmanageable.	Dishonesty	Honesty	Hypervigilance
2. Came to believe that a Power greater than ourselves could restore us to sanity.	Despair	Hope	Idealism
3. Made a decision to turn our will and our lives over to the care of God *as we understood Him.*	Doubt	Faith	Gullibility
4. Made a searching and fearless moral inventory of ourselves.	Cowardice	Courage	Recklessness
5. Admitted to God, to ourselves, and to another human being the exact nature of our wrongs.	Deceit	Integrity	Self-righteousness
6. Were entirely ready to have God remove all these defects of character.	Control	Willingness	Subservience
7. Humbly asked Him to remove our shortcomings.	Arrogance	Humility	Worthlessness

(Continued)

† Principles are listed in Pittman, *Practice These Principles*, with two variations: compassion (instead of brotherly love) and accountability (instead of justice). Both align more closely with character literature and use in work environments.

STEP	DEFICIENCY (too little)	PRINCIPLE	EXCESS (too much)
8. Made a list of all persons we had harmed, and became willing to make amends to them all.	Apathy	Compassion	Agony
9. Made direct amends to such people wherever possible, except when to do so would injure them or others.	Irresponsibility	Accountability	Manipulation
10. Continued to take personal inventory and when we were wrong promptly admitted it.	Laziness	Perseverance	Perfectionism
11. Sought through prayer and meditation to improve our conscious contact with God *as we understood Him*, praying only for knowledge of His will for us and the power to carry that out.	Self-absorption	Spiritual Awareness	Fundamentalism
12. Having had a spiritual awakening as the result of these Steps, we tried to carry this message to _____, and to practice these principles in all our affairs.	Ingratitude	Service	Suffocation

Learning balance and judgment are critical to our recovery. I've heard people say, "My picker is broken," meaning they make bad relationship choices. We can probably say the same about workplaces. But as we get further in our development, we become more discerning and hone our judgment. Our decisions are never made in isolation. No longer the self-centered people we were, we now consider how our actions affect others in the long term. The goal is to develop serenity, even as we teeter, or stand firmly, on the narrow ridge trying to find our balance.

We Strive for "Emotional Sobriety"

In a 1958 essay, AA cofounder Bill Wilson described the benefits of "emotional sobriety" as more maturity, peace, and joy. Despite years of sobriety, he was plagued with depression and dependency on externalities: "people or circumstances to supply me with prestige, security, and the like."[16] Work is an easy target for our dependencies. It sometimes satisfies but inevitably disappoints, giving us a ready excuse to feel offended or rejected and to fall back into addiction.

With emotional sobriety, we're less reactive and ruled by our emotions. We work with all kinds of people, some enormously frustrating and annoying. Some are flat-out jerks, mean and vindictive. But we don't set out to change others. We can't manifest a more productive coworker, more reasonable customer, or more understanding boss. The Adult Children of Alcoholics and Dysfunctional Families' secular version of the Serenity Prayer makes that clear: "Today, I seek the serenity to accept the people I cannot change, the courage to change the one I can, and the wisdom to know that one is me."[17]

Through the stories, exploration, and reflection questions in this book, you'll gain more than knowledge. You'll have new tools to use in both your professional and personal life to deepen your recovery and strengthen your character. Over time, you'll develop resilience, but you'll go beyond merely resisting adversity and landing on your feet. You'll become more agile—able to adapt to unknown situations and tackle any difficult work situation you face with dexterity and confidence throughout your career.

SECTION 1

We Accept External Guidance

STEP	DEFICIENCY (too little)	PRINCIPLE	EXCESS (too much)
1. We admitted we were powerless over _____ —that our lives had become unmanageable.	Dishonesty	Honesty	Hypervigilance
2. Came to believe that a Power greater than ourselves could restore us to sanity.	Despair	Hope	Idealism
3. Made a decision to turn our will and our lives over to the care of God *as we understood Him.*	Doubt	Faith	Gullibility

When we first entered recovery, we admitted that we had a problem—that alcohol, drugs, social media, gambling, shopping, food, sex, work, or other addictions or compulsive behaviors caused problems in our life and made work difficult or impossible. We recognized that we could not stop our addictive use or behaviors on our own and began to trust and accept guidance from others. We accessed power beyond ourselves.

During the first three steps of a Twelve Step program, the principles of honesty, hope, and faith are most important. In a work environment, we become the kind of employee others want as a team member: ethical, optimistic, and trustworthy. At work, as in recovery, we develop skills in accessing what we need. We stress less, knowing we can't change everything we would like to and, instead, accept people and conditions as they are. With outside perspectives, less rigidity, and a more reliable intuition, we get better at discerning what to do, or what not to do, in difficult situations.

CHAPTER 1

Honesty

Chapter Overview

Our first step in recovery was admitting our addiction—being honest with ourselves. Since taking that step, we no longer need to protect our ego and have developed a conscience. We aren't dishonest with ourselves or with others, and we use judgment about how much to share to avoid hypervigilance.

Kareem's Dilemma

When we look for a new job, some of us are haunted by our past and struggle with how much to reveal. Here's Kareem's story:

I'm looking for work after a two-year hiatus. I know I'll be asked during the interview about the employment gap. I was using and drinking pretty heavily and in rehab during some of that time.

I'm going to see how comfortable I feel with the interviewer, but I'm thinking of saying, "I was in rehab for a while for an addiction, but I've been clean and sober for six months now." Or I might keep it vague and say, "Let's call it a mental health break," or "I needed some time away from work to focus on myself."

I'd rather be honest about the rehab. If that doesn't fit for the company, then maybe the company is not a good fit for me. If it's a hostile environment, then I don't want to be there. My view is when people are honest, then you know you can trust them even if they had a tough past. If I tell the truth about my history, then why would I lie about anything else?

Applying for a job tests our honesty and is a window into other difficult decisions we make about how we present ourselves. Having admitted our addiction in Step One, we face more nuance about how honest we want to be at work.

Honesty at Work

Honesty means telling the truth. In recovery, we decide how to represent ourselves in sincere and thorough ways and are honest with ourselves.

Telling the Truth

Any Twelve Step program first asks us to be honest. The Alcoholics Anonymous (AA) website lists questions with these instructions: "Below are some questions we tried to answer honestly."[1] When we admitted we were powerless over our addiction, we accepted hard truths we may have been denying for a long time. We were "sick and tired of being sick and tired," as we hear in the rooms of recovery.

At its core, honesty means telling the truth. In active addiction, we couldn't trust ourselves, and we weren't trustworthy. Even when his hangover was obvious, Ben, a delivery driver, had a dozen ready excuses for being late to work: His car broke down, he had to help someone, or he wasn't feeling well. Every day, we have chances to be truthful at work. We account for our time, track expenses, and report on our accomplishments.

Honest Appraisal

Kareem wants to end his history of lying and tell the truth about his past struggles. He follows the path of a semiconductor researcher at Intel, who shared his story:

> I was terrified to tell HR, or anyone really, about my past. But I preferred honesty… I wanted to be upfront and transparent, but it was a terrifying leap of faith. To my shock, the hiring manager said, "We're more concerned with what you've been

doing recently than what happened in the past." I remember those words very, very vividly. It set me free from a paralyzing fear that gripped me for over a decade—the best feeling of my life.[2]

In AA literature, program founders ask us to take an "honest appraisal,"[3] to consider whether we have an "honest desire,"[4] and to make an "honest effort."[5] In this sense, they want us to be sincere and thorough. A mechanic gives an honest appraisal to estimate repair costs. Managers give an honest appraisal when they give feedback to their direct reports. For Kareem, an honest appraisal means assessing whether the work environment will be accepting and supportive. Will they value his honesty? Will they accept him?

One way to develop honesty is to prepare for likely questions. When interviewing a job candidate, a hiring manager may ask any of the following:

- Tell me about a big mistake you made in a previous job.
- Tell me about a time when you weren't completely honest.
- Why did you leave your previous job?
- What did you do during the gap between your last two jobs?
- Tell me about a conflict you had with someone at work.

Practice answering these questions, so you're ready when the time comes. Choose responses that are relevant to the position, illustrate your qualifications, and reflect well on you. When you answer, you can sound natural without coming across as though you're reading a script.

Honesty With Ourselves

Honesty also means taking a good, hard look at ourselves. For 22 years, Donna stayed in a job she coasted in. She said she liked the job: "It's great for me. My boss doesn't want to get anything done, and I don't do anything." Only after she landed a new job did she admit how unhappy she was, contributing so little to the organization.

In my first job out of college, at a bank, my manager asked me to call the president's assistant. I was nervous and stumbled over my words.

She was short with me, which sent me into a puddle, sobbing uncontrollably in the bathroom. Desperately seeking approval from others, I couldn't take what felt like ridicule and rejection.

Being honest with ourselves means knowing our triggers and taking responsibility for our reactions. The president's assistant was a little mean, but of course, I overreacted. Over time, we learn which triggers are based on fears we need to face. We learn what we're defending or protecting, which might be something about ourselves that we haven't fully accepted or been honest about. With a more honest self-assessment, we can choose to react differently in situations that push those buttons.

Dishonesty: Too Little Honesty

Most people believe that lying for selfish reasons is wrong, immoral, and unethical. In recovery, we don't intentionally mislead or deceive people with false information.

People lie to protect their ego—to avoid negative consequences, succumbing to their fears instead of walking through them. We're afraid of disappointing others, not measuring up, losing a connection, or being left out. We lie to seem more attractive, to gain status, or to belong.[6] Those of us with addiction issues lied to ourselves about whether we were *really* addicted.

Twelve Step programs ask us to be "rigorously honest."[7] What does that mean at work? It could mean we don't use excuses to lie. We don't pad expense accounts because "I deserve more pay," steal because "everyone does it," or skim product off the top because "no one would ever notice." That last reason—not getting caught—makes dishonesty tempting, but it's the lowest form of moral reasoning.[8]

Lying by omission, or withholding or concealing information critical to a job, is still lying. A blatant example is working two full-time remote jobs without telling either employer. A more subtle example is Kareem's employer telling him that overtime averages only five hours per week, but not saying that a big project is coming up that requires much more.

Indirect communication may be dishonest. People may feel manipulated by the "sandwich" way of giving feedback: Start with good news, slide the bad news in the middle, and end on a positive note. Often, employees miss the feedback entirely.[9] When companies communicate layoffs, employees prefer the news directly; they know it's coming anyway.[10]

An HR manager tried to talk with an employee about her work attire. She was so subtle, suggesting that she dress more "professionally," that the woman didn't get the point. After a few more tries, the HR manager finally blurted out, "Your boobs are hanging out!" The woman immediately said, "Oh! I didn't realize. Thank you for telling me."

I'm not suggesting you do this at work! Good communication takes skills that we develop over time and come to trust with experience. The situation and audience always help us determine the best communication approach. After years of active addiction, perhaps in isolation, many of us need outside perspectives to find the right balance.

Being too blunt can be as dishonest as being too subtle. Saying, "To be honest" or "I'm just being honest," and then proceeding to say whatever is on your mind is usually self-serving and not considerate of the other. Those phrases aren't universal excuses for harsh negative feedback or an unwanted sexual remark.

Hypervigilance: Too Much Honesty

How many of us download an app and click the box to agree, "I have read the terms and conditions," when we haven't? Perfect honesty isn't always practical.

Sometimes, we tell "white lies" to avoid hurting people's feelings, putting ourselves in uncomfortable situations, avoiding conflict, or wasting time. Although technically lies, these false statements are typically thought of as insignificant.[11] They can benefit the person telling them or the receiver, but the impact is low.[12]

You might tell a white lie as an expected social nicety.[13] You might say, "It was good to meet you too" when it wasn't, or "I hope to see you again too," when you don't. Failing to respond could be awkward and considered hypervigilant.

For a more obvious example of hypervigilance, imagine that Kareem gave his interviewer the gory details of his addiction: his "drugalog," the work altercations, and his multiple relapses. We could call this oversharing or giving too much information (TMI). We get the same incredulous stares when we launch into a long story about why we're late or why we miss a deadline. A short explanation is enough: "It took me longer than I thought to make the uptown deliveries," or "I didn't realize how long it would take accounting to pull the data." Otherwise, we make the situation worse by tripping over ourselves trying to make things right.

A hypervigilant deli worker tells a customer that the ham will be thrown out tomorrow if it's not sold. A hypervigilant software vendor describes, in detail, a bug that was just fixed. If you're confident that the ham is good today and the software works now, you don't need to hurt yourself or your business. Kareem doesn't need to say, "I might have a relapse." Unfortunately, that's true for all of us, and an employer already knows it.

When communicating, we consider how much detail the receiver needs to know. A manager doesn't have to point out every little thing an employee did wrong during a presentation. Two or three areas to work on are enough. Believing it's dishonest to leave out minor missteps, a hypervigilant manager overwhelms and discourages the employee from making any changes at all. In a sense, hypervigilance shows our dishonest, distorted judgment about ourselves and those around us. We need to trust our ability to communicate just enough for the receiver to understand us and to get what they need from what we say.

The Narrow Ridge of Honesty

Work culture challenges us to find middle ground without going to extremes and to consider our motives. Although white lies are usually acceptable, like altruistic lies, they may have negative consequences. In the end, what's ethical is judged by those affected.

Work Cultures

In most work environments, we're expected to represent our best selves and place our work in the best possible light. On LinkedIn, we highlight our accomplishments and omit our failures. Marketers emphasize the best aspects of their product or service and don't mention better aspects of competitors' products. Within some industries or professionals, exaggeration is not only acceptable but encouraged. Entrepreneurs may be expected to inflate their potential customer base or business valuation. In recovery, taking rigorous honesty too far in these situations may cost us a job, a customer, or an investor.

We have to be savvy—to assess the context of where we work and how others behave. But we don't follow clearly unethical behavior just because it's normalized. In active addiction, it may have been difficult to avoid going along with others, but we're stronger now.

Navigating difficult work situations requires a look inside ourselves, an external perspective, and then a decision about how to act or respond. You might consider your own character, the context of the situation, and your message by answering these questions:

- Character: What do I want to accomplish for myself—both short and long terms? What impact do I want to have? How do I want to be perceived? What fears or character weaknesses may get in the way of my being rigorously honest? How can I withstand the potential negative consequences?
- Context: Who is affected by my action or decision? How much do people need to know? How do others act in similar situations? What external guidance can I seek (e.g., company guidelines, my boss, a higher power)?
- Message: Having thought through my character and the context, what can I say and do that is honest—neither lying nor hypervigilant? How should I communicate what I need to communicate? Can I have a conversation in person instead of by text or email? How can my tone and timing convey my sincerity?[14]

White and Altruistic Lies

Although acceptable in situations described earlier, white lies are a murky area. If a white lie benefits you, you may question your motives and rethink what you'll say. Organizations encourage conformity, and we tend to go along with what others say whether we agree or not. But rigorous honesty guides us to err on the side of truth even if it means discomfort.

Lies of greater consequence that benefit others are called altruistic lies. For example, a doctor might downplay the causes of a disease to preserve a patient's feelings about their past behavior. Although considered ethical, altruistic lies can cause problems in working environments. Under the guise of benefitting the organization rather than themselves, leaders lie in these types of situations:

- Withholding information in a crisis situation to maintain the company's image, while causing more reputational damage once the information is revealed
- Delaying telling employees about an office move to keep employees as long as possible, but leaving them too little time to find other work
- Downplaying morale issues during job interviews to hire the best talent, but setting a new employee up for a negative experience

These situations are narrow-ridge dilemmas because of the tension between ourselves and others. What seems like a good business decision for the company ultimately does more harm.

Another downside of altruistic lying is that people may be more prone to other types of lies in the future.[15] Lies become easier, and over time, people become less trustworthy. Those of us in recovery know how easily little lies become big lies. The expression "lies beget lies" warns how one lie often requires others. A sales manager who lies about a product launch date may have to lie again when the customer asks why the product isn't available. Then she'll invent technical or supply chain issues to explain the delay.

Judgments of Honesty

The law, operational guidelines, codes of conduct, ethics boards, and the HR department may serve as workplace authorities of whether a lie was justified. But in recovery, we develop a conscience, build skills, and tell the truth. We don't need official rules to tell us how to be honest.

The balance of too little and too much honesty—like all principles in practice—depends on our good judgment. We decide what, how much, and when disclosure is appropriate, and we practice restraint when it's not appropriate. During the job interview, Kareem can strike this balance by briefly telling the truth about his work gap, and then transitioning to more positive information. He can focus on what he enjoyed about his previous job and what he's looking forward to. He can mention that his previous employer agreed to be a reference for him. As he decides what to say, Kareem also considers how long he's been out of work and in recovery, how badly he needs the job, how tight the job market is, how the interview is going so far, and so on.

Once Kareem gets hired, if he's asked out to drinks with coworkers, how much does he need to say? He can say, "No, thanks. I've got to get home." If asked repeatedly or pushed ("C'mon. We're all going."), he can say that he doesn't drink. If he's still pushed, he can say, "If I start, I'll never stop," or "I'm in recovery," or just, "No, really, thanks, anyway." All responses are honest, and all are along the narrow ridge—that uncomfortable place he's balancing to avoid lying or saying more than he wants or needs to.

Closing Thoughts

The Alcoholics Anonymous description of "How It Works" warns that people who fail in the Twelve Step program are "constitutionally incapable of being honest with themselves. There are such unfortunates."[16] This is harsh, but we relate because we have spent time in that space—where we could not be fully honest with ourselves—and the results may have propelled us into recovery.

But now we are fortunate. We're in recovery, and we're employable. Without being foolishly hypervigilant, we tell the truth in ways that honor our commitment to live better lives. By practicing rigorous honesty with ourselves and with others, we "let the chips fall where they may," as the saying goes. Yes, we might suffer negative consequences, but we walk through our fears and, over time, strengthen our character enough that we can accept the consequences and have no reason to lie.

Reflection Questions

1. Describe a time when you admired someone's honesty at work. What did they say or do? What positive and negative results did they experience? How did their skill differ from yours?

2. When have you been rigorously honest? Think about a few times in your work life when others may have said that you modeled this principle well. What unexpected—both positive and negative—consequences came from this experience?

3. Think about a time when you were dishonest at work. What would you do differently today?

4. Think about a time when you were hypervigilant about honesty at work. What would you do differently today?

5. Answer the questions about character, context, and message in this chapter to work through a current situation. What do you decide based on your answers?

CHAPTER 2

Hope

Chapter Overview

Hope is a mainstay of recovery—believing that a good future is possible. We make goals, identify pathways, and take action, yet remain open, allowing opportunities to emerge and adapting as they do. We stay clear of despair, which is a symptom of depression, and idealism, or wishful thinking, which sets us up for failure. Although opposites in some ways, hope and pessimism can be held simultaneously along the narrow ridge.

Jade's Dilemma

Entrepreneurs know the importance of hope. Here's Jade's story about starting a new business:

About a year into recovery, I decided to start a business leading workshops to help people connect with their bodies. The idea is for people, through movement, to feel grounded in their bodies, which often leads to personal development and insight. As an entrepreneur, I constantly walk this line of feeling like I'm doing this great thing that's going to really take off and feeling like a total failure.

I am hoping for the best. I rented a dance studio, and I spend a lot of time promoting events by email and on Facebook. Sometimes, I feel deflated when only a couple of people show up, but I'm trying to get better at just focusing on them and their experience. People tell me what an amazing impact the experience has had on them, but I want to expand my reach.

I'm trying to be realistic. Maybe I need to do something other than direct marketing and partner with existing organizations and events. I don't know. It's taking a lot for me to stay positive.

Jade says she is "hoping for the best." Hope drives Step Two, "Came to believe that a Power greater than ourselves could restore us to sanity." After Step One, when we admitted we were powerless, we started believing that we have a future, one worth planning for.

Hope at Work

Hope involves thinking, feeling, and action and is essential for a successful career. We practice hope by letting go of preconceptions and approaching each situation with more of a beginner's mind—identifying pathways toward goals and working to achieve them. Spirituality is important for us to be hopeful; we accept a world beyond our comprehension and control.

Hope and Optimism

In most Twelve Step programs, we're asked "to share our experience, strength, and hope."[1] Hope may be defined as, "the belief that the future will be better than the present, along with the belief that you have the power to make it so."[2] Hope is an emotion and a posture, or position, we take: We can choose to be hopeful. Even in the worst of times, we accept that we can't comprehend or control everything around us and allow ourselves to imagine the possibility and feel of a better future, even if we don't know how, what, or why that may happen.

Without hope, Jade couldn't get it together to market her business. She believes that her actions will affect future outcomes. In active addiction, many of us felt hopeless, as though it didn't matter what we said or did; the outcome would be the same. In recovery, we know that our actions can affect outcomes.

Hope requires action, which distinguishes it from optimism. Optimism also means having a positive outlook, but it doesn't involve any steps toward future outcomes.[3]

Professor, author, and activist Cornel West describes hope as a collective action: "Hope is about everybody trying to contribute to the push, the motion, the momentum, the movement for something bigger than them that's better. The good, the beautiful. If you're not in motion, you're a spectator."[4] Without action, we may have wishful thinking. You may want a promotion, but without a plan and hard work, you're less likely to get one. Hope increases our chances of success, including career success.[5]

Having hope means discovering goals, pathways to achieve them, and agency to follow through.[6] As we set goals for our work and for our careers, we identify multiple paths, or ways, to achieve them, which further increases our chance of success.

Hope, Resilience, and Agility

Having hope also means being realistic and reassessing goals when necessary.[7] Circumstances may change, so our goals may need to be adjusted. We identify specific goals, but not so specific that we limit the possibility of success. More important is being open to seeing new opportunities as they arise. Then, we form a new goal to seize them. Hope isn't attached to any specific outcome.

Constantly reclarifying, or recharting a somewhat meandering path, leads us beyond resilience. Resilience is important to withstand pressure but isn't enough for long-term career success. We also practice adapting, so when circumstances change, which they always do, we're ready to change, too, and still maintain hope.

After getting a degree in data analytics, a high-demand field when she started school, Marguerite found herself without a job when she graduated. Tech was downsizing, so she had to adjust her goals. She worked for a smaller company in another city until market conditions changed. Then, she got a job more in line, although not perfectly aligned, with her original goal. Hope is a driver—both of her willingness to change her goals and for her to keep working toward a new goal.

As the saying goes, "We plan, God laughs." Whatever your idea of a higher power, we know that we can't possibly control every outcome. Still, we prepare for obstacles as best we can. We build detours into the plans, ready to deal with what's in our way. Creative problem solving—tackling obstacles and getting out of difficult situations—is a key component of hope.[8] Just as we learn in recovery, we face obstacles but don't let them stymie us. The more we handle, the more agile we become, managing the unexpected with greater ease until we barely notice the minor problems.

No one I know says the process of abstaining from an addiction is a straight path. When we face cravings, setbacks, or relapse, we just keep going. That is hope.

Hope Outside Ourselves

In Step Two, we "came to believe that a Power greater than ourselves could restore us to sanity." This is the first step in the program that gently ("came to believe") eases people toward spirituality. At some dark point in our lives, we may have made our addictive substance our higher power. I mentioned earlier that I also made my employer my higher power. I relied on the company to guide my actions, some of which negatively affected my personal life.

In Step Two, we're asked to consider something else. We're invited to look outside ourselves for help. As a spiritual skill, hope is part of transcendence, connecting to something larger than ourselves that gives us meaning.[9]

Spiritual beliefs are important to hope, and that belief may take many forms. A higher power means many different things to people in Twelve Step programs: nature, a Christian God, oxygen, others in recovery, reality—the list goes on. Some people think of it more as a greater or a deeper power or something within themselves, like their higher self or intuition. Also, what people identify can change over time, and some have more than one higher power. In fact, multiple sources of a spiritual belief are best for sustaining hope.[10]

In a working environment, a higher power can be anything that guides us. This can be written guidelines, for example, an organizational mission or vision, policies or procedures, a job description, a customer bill of rights, or a code of ethics. Or a higher power may be people you trust and consult: your manager, a union representative, someone in HR, or a coworker. In recovery, having multiple outside forces to guide us—for example, a sponsor, fellow travelers, trusted advisors, and program steps and principles—keeps us grounded, and stops us from falling into despair, which we'll explore next.

Despair: Too Little Hope

Having too little hope is hopelessness, or despair. A dangerous place for people in recovery, despair can be caused by or can fuel distorted or negative thinking. Former addicts know as well as anyone the dangers of despair, or believing that a desired outcome isn't possible—that nothing we do will make a difference. Feelings of hopelessness can spiral into self-pity. As I heard in a meeting, "Poor me, poor me, pour me a drink." We become victims who can't see our role in creating a problem or in solving it, so we fall back on our addictions—our default ways of coping. We also can't see clearly because we may too easily trust our own vision: We see the future, and it is *bad*.

Despair is a "core symptom of depression."[11] "Deaths of despair," from "drug overdoses, suicide, and alcoholic liver disease" have risen dramatically since the 1950s and contributed to the United States' declining life expectancy.[12] Scholars blame economic conditions affecting the working class.[13] Work can be a despairing place.

Like hope, despair can be cognitive, behavioral, or emotional. In cognitive despair, we're embroiled in thoughts of worthlessness, guilt, and shame. These thoughts might be linked to distortions, for example, focusing too much on short-term rather than long-term outcomes, or believing others to be more hostile than they are. A sideways glance from a coworker or seeing two coworkers whispering leads to our "stinking thinking," as we hear in the rooms of recovery. Spinning up negative thoughts about ourselves, our old, self-centered thinking could get in the way of hope.

Behavioral despair refers to actions taken because we don't care about the future. We might be reckless or impulsive, familiar ways of behaving in active addiction. Part of a prison return-to-work program, Valerie quit in a huff over a political debate. Later, she said the program saved her life but, at the time, she saw no good outcomes.

When we *feel* despair, we may be sad, irritable, lonely, or tired. We lack motivation. We drag ourselves out of bed to go to work.

Two of those emotions—lonely and tired—may look familiar. A tool we're taught in recovery is "HALT." If we feel triggered or emotionally unregulated, we check with ourselves to see whether one of four stressors is causing the problem: Are we **h**ungry? **A**ngry? **L**onely? **T**ired?[14] The questions help us pause—another helpful recovery tool—and the answers help us figure out what to do. How can we manage our emotions or cope when problems arise?

The physical stressors, being hungry and tired, have obvious fixes. Working through lunch is often expected at work, a badge of honor and loyalty. But prioritizing our recovery means prioritizing what our bodies need so we can be successful at work.

Anger and loneliness are more complicated, but recovery tools, for example, Step Four (analyzing our resentments) and going to meetings or calling others in recovery, can help. However we answer the HALT questions, they put us back in control as we develop new skills. We can make choices that can save us from feelings of despair.

Idealism: Too Much Hope

We can't be too hopeful, as an emotional state, but we can be idealistic. Idealism can cause problems, reminding us of the insanity of our time in active addiction. When we are hopeful, we believe in a "reasonable chance" of a positive outcome.[15] We don't *really* know the odds, so we don't really know what is "reasonable," but we choose to feel more open than closed to future possibilities.

When we're idealistic, we're not realistic about the future; we strive for ideals—a narrow definition of a future we control. Despite evidence, we're unwilling to believe that a desired outcome won't likely happen. Andrew Chignell, who studies hope, calls this "bad hope"—ignoring obvious signs or data and, as a result, failing to act.[16] This is when hope becomes poisonous, distorting our understanding and preventing us from engaging the world as it is.

Katrina worked as a housekeeper for a hotel in Chicago. Not seeing the "writing on the wall," she trained contractors from another company to do her job. The hotel then outsourced all housekeeping jobs and laid off Katrina and her coworkers. She was offered a job with the contracting firm but at a much lower wage. In this situation, Katrina may have had no choice, but her failure to see the inevitable is an example of her idealism.

The expression "hoping against hope" means remaining hopeful despite obstacles. This is a positive way of being—to a point. In the *Alcoholics Anonymous* "Big Book," we read, "At first some of us tried to avoid the issue, hoping against hope we were not true alcoholics."[17] We didn't face reality. Some obstacles *are* insurmountable. We need to recognize when problem solving is futile and, instead, adjust our goals so we're more likely to achieve them.

If Jade's dance business becomes a financial burden, she may need to close up shop. Entrepreneurs often go into debt to fund a business, but they have to weigh the costs. In addition to financial costs, maybe they're losing family time because of long hours, or they're missing other work opportunities. At some point, founders evaluate the chance of success against the casualties to other aspects of their life.

Changing directions doesn't necessarily mean failure. If Jade's venture fails, she can apply what she learned and start a new business when another idea strikes and the time is right.

Step Two invites us to seek help to "restore us to sanity." Doing the same things over and over and over in active addiction and expecting different outcomes was insane. Thinking we could stop at one drink, eat one cookie, go to one store and not buy anything—whatever our addiction—was not something we could will ourselves to change.

At work, insanity could be looking at the same spreadsheet for hours, trying to get a formula to run; at some point, we have to stop and walk away. Powers greater than ourselves are family members who tell us to come home or a manager who reminds us that the problem doesn't have to be solved today.

Appropriately, Chignell warns about hope becoming "an opiate rather than a motivator."[18] We're in trouble when we obsess about something that may or may not happen and lose sight of other things that require our attention. A fantasy world isn't a healthy place to live.

Excessive optimism also may leave us unprepared for the future. We're shocked when things go wrong—when we finally face, as Katrina did, that the outcome is not good. At that point, we're forced to adjust our plans, but we're in a weaker position to accept what comes.

The Narrow Ridge of Hope

Without falling into despair or getting carried away with grand plans that will never be, we hold hope even in hard times. Distinguishing between short- and long-term success and accurately assessing information keep us centered in hope.

Hope, Skepticism, and Pessimism

Along the narrow ridge, we hope for the best but prepare for the worst. We don't know what's going to happen, but we can roll with whatever does.

Andrew Chignell doesn't believe that hope must be realistic. He believes we can be hopeful about a possibility, however unlikely. We are hopeful, yet skeptical and questioning. Hope may include both a sense of wonder about the future and a suspicion about outcomes.[19] When we take a new job, we feel both joy about our career advancement and apprehension about whether we'll fit in. We hold conflicting feelings along the narrow ridge without getting carried away by one or the other.

Even in the worst of times, as in early recovery, we can maintain hope. Chignell describes "understandable, justified pessimism,"[20] based on, for example, world events or market conditions that affect our job prospects. The "deaths of despair" discussed earlier make career success seem hopeless. But we can be pessimistic and still hopeful that things could turn out well, combining both. Despite our doubts about a good outcome, we're still active, engaged participants in life. Even in early recovery, we dragged ourselves to meetings hoping for a better solution than our addiction.

Put another way, Cornel West notes the paradoxical but essential relationship between hope and despair: "Those who have never despaired have neither lived nor loved. Hope is inseparable from despair.

Those of us who truly hope make despair a constant companion whom we outwrestle every day owing to our commitment to justice, love, and hope."[21] West describes the importance of facing our fears to become stronger, more productive people. Despair is a motivational force for a better life for ourselves and those around us.

Short and Long Terms

Distinguishing between short- and long-term wins helps avoid wild swings between believing all is lost and all is perfect. These swings cause an emotional rollercoaster that leaves us worn out and wondering which end is up. Of course, keeping this perspective is difficult, particularly when every dollar counts. One lost customer could mean that a small business owner can't make payroll. An engine problem could mean that a delivery driver can't pay rent.

The skill is riding the short-term waves while maintaining hope for the long term. A work setback is just that—a setback. With a growth mindset, we believe that learning from short-term disappointments fuels our long-term goals. As we develop hope, we welcome setbacks as learning opportunities.

When Yael's entire marketing team was laid off—except her—she worked 14-hour days to pick up the slack. She did that for a short time, hoping that conditions would change and she could rehire staff. Skeptical about getting things done every day, she focused on solving problems and learning new skills, while keeping a long view of possibilities for the future. In the end, her work paid off. Business picked up, she was able to hire, and her work—and her hopeful attitude—was rewarded with a promotion.

To plan for a long, successful career, you may begin with a vision of your future self. Think about times in your life when you felt you were at your best. Jot down notes about each situation, what you did, and the impact on or reactions from others. Next, ask three people who know you well to identify your top three strengths. Finally, imagine you're winning an award from your company or from a community organization. What would someone say about you? Include future examples that illustrate your effect on individuals' work or personal lives; your contribution to the team, your company, and your community; and the values you hold and model for others. Hold this vision with hope.

Accurate Assessments

In work environments, we're challenged to accurately assess information. Developing a budget requires us to consider what we'll need in the future and how much we can reasonably earn to pay for it. Setting production goals requires us to consider materials, labor, and other costs. When do we include a new piece of equipment as a capital expense in the budget? We might budget only for ongoing maintenance, hopeful that the equipment won't need to be replaced. We may be wrong.

We walk the narrow ridge of hope and skepticism by relying on experience and looking at multiple sources of information. A more optimistic sales manager might overestimate revenue, while a more pessimistic manager might underestimate revenue. We aren't perfect predictors of the future, which is why we need a realistic outlook and a hopeful heart.

Closing Thoughts

All recovery programs are programs of hope. We believe that we can make it through another day without succumbing to our addiction, and we believe in a better future. But wishful thinking isn't enough: Positive action makes the difference.

Working the steps and going to meetings—and going to work—are acts of hope. Despair keeps us isolated, and idealism sets us up for disappointment. Hope swells within communities, creating possibilities that wouldn't otherwise exist. By developing hope in ourselves, we can be part of the movement.

Reflection Questions

1. Do you consider yourself a hopeful person? Can you relax into a crisis and set aside anxiety and fear long enough to see clearly?

2. Do you set career goals, identify pathways, and take action, yet allow for change? How helpful or unhelpful do you find the process?

3. What are some times in your life when you felt particularly hopeful? What contributed to your feelings and actions? Consider your own contributions, not just external circumstances. How might you create those feelings and actions in times when external circumstances are difficult?

4. When have you felt despair? What helped you get through those feelings?

5. What is a time when you felt that you weren't realistic in thinking about your career? What got in the way of your accurately assessing possible outcomes?

CHAPTER 3

Faith

Chapter Overview

In Step Three, we "made a decision," allowing an opening to believe in something outside ourselves. We find strength and comfort in relaxing into whatever may be. With confidence in ourselves and in the world around us, we avoid doubt and gullibility: We're neither too worried about the future nor too easily manipulated.

Malcolm's Dilemma

When faced with a potential job layoff or termination, we can either worry ourselves sick or take things as they come. Here's Malcolm's story:

During the COVID-19 pandemic, I landed a job as a contact tracer. I loved the work, and it paid well for a contract job— more money than I ever made. I had flexible hours and felt like I was doing something important: interviewing people, tracking down possible cases, and providing resources for people who were exposed to the virus.

After a few months, mask mandates and vaccines became more prevalent, and the U.S. government needed fewer contact tracers. Then came the job cuts. I was spared during several rounds of layoffs. But it was such a stressful time because I knew it was coming. I just didn't know when.

Finally, I was laid off, and then I had to decide whether to go on unemployment. It was a lot of paperwork, and what if I got a new job quickly and didn't need it? I was worried this whole time, not knowing what to do.

Malcolm felt *hopeful* that his job would continue even though surviving more rounds of layoffs was unlikely. Taking lessons from Step Two, he embraced a reality he didn't fully understand or control. Then, he needed *faith* to get through the coming months.

Faith at Work

Like hope, faith is a belief about reality without conclusive proof or clear evidence. When we make a decision to choose faith, we choose to fully trust in outside forces that orient us to be actively engaged in our lives. With this grounding, we use the skills we have and develop new ones that are essential to a successful career and a successful life. Mindfulness practices keep us focused on the moment instead of stressing about what we can't control.

"Made a Decision"

Raised in a third- (and possibly fourth-) generation atheist household, I've struggled with the concept of faith. Step Three was the hardest for me and the most valuable in my life. I never thought that the concept of a higher power could be helpful to me—a guide and a source of comfort. I learned that the object of our faith doesn't matter; what's important is that we accept that *we* are not God. In Step One, we admitted that we couldn't manage our own lives—that we needed help. We couldn't trust ourselves, so we looked outside ourselves for guidance.

Step Three is cleverly written—"Made a decision"—for addicts and alcoholics to *consider* faith. I looked for a Step 3.5 that would tell me what and how to believe. But we don't have to identify anything at all. The list of possible higher, or greater, powers in Chapter 2 are just ideas. I asked a devout Catholic friend for her concept of God, and she said she doesn't think of God as a concept. She experiences a direct relationship with God, as do many people in Twelve Step programs. For me, I have a vague concept not tied to a religious tradition, and I am working on how I experience a world I can't define or understand.

Faith and hope are related—both about believing in something and holding it as valued without decisive proof or incontrovertible evidence.

Hope is also an emotion, focused on future outcomes and taking steps toward them, while faith is broader. Faith is about acceptance of what's ahead, regardless of outcomes. We have faith that, even if things don't go our way, we'll be OK. As we hear in recovery, we "live life on life's terms." We feel confident (derived from "with" and "trust"[1]) that we already have, can build, will be able to access, or will be provided the skills we'll need to manage through.

Trust at Work

Trust is related to faith but, unlike faith, is based on observations or experience. We trust our employer, which means we rely on them to follow through on commitments. If you didn't trust that you would get paid on Friday, why would you show up on Monday? We also trust in ourselves and the people we work with because we know our history of doing the work. As we use the skills we have and develop new skills, our *faith* grows, even though we don't have evidence about what's next. Having faith in a team means we can relax, knowing that people will likely come through when needed. We trust people as they are, not how we want them to be.

Faith helps us accept what we can't control. Typically, Twelve Step meetings start with the Serenity Prayer, which encourages acceptance: "God, grant me the serenity to accept the things I cannot change."[2] The moody coworker, the redundant process, the boring tasks—we put up with a lot at work. Naturally, we like some parts of our jobs more than others. Flailing against things we don't like ("If I were in charge…") accomplishes nothing and harms only ourselves.

Trusting that our work has meaning puts minor work annoyances and inconveniences in perspective. What's the bigger picture of your job for you, personally? Why are you working? Are you supporting a family, getting out of debt, or striving for a better job? What's the bigger picture of your job for the organization? What does your organization do that makes you feel accomplished? How do you contribute to company goals or client satisfaction? This perspective is one way of thinking about faith: It's the intangibles that we don't see but know exist and are worth working toward.

Mindfulness

Kevin Griffin, author of *One Breath at a Time: Buddhism and the Twelve Steps*, views "making a decision" as a commitment to a spiritual path and the most important part of Step Three.[3] He describes the value of mindfulness as the first step of meditation—practicing nonreactivity, or distinguishing between our thoughts and reality.[4] Without judgment, we focus on our sensations and the environment in the present moment to gain clarity and perspective. In the workplace, this focus helps us respond to situations more skillfully, with less self-centered, distorted thinking. As Malcolm waits for a decision about his job status, he's able to concentrate on his responsibilities without too much distraction about what may happen in the future.

Benefits of mindfulness for individuals and organizations are well documented. Reduced stress, better sleep, less pain, and higher productivity inspire corporate initiatives for mindfulness practices in the workplace.[5] Managers may encourage employees to take a mindfulness break for just two minutes a day, observing their breath and surroundings and keeping a gratitude journal, as Google has new employees do.[6] Although 20 minutes is a common recommendation for daily meditation, 13 minutes a day for 8 weeks has significant benefits for mood, memory, attention, and anxiety.[7]

Many work situations can cause us stress. But if you have an important meeting and your child is sick, you're either going to make the meeting or not. You have no control, so you might as well just focus on the moment. A friend described mindfulness as tapping into a quiet place within herself, wherever she is. We trust that things will work out, for the most part, because we have no better option. We remind ourselves that "this too shall pass" and do what we can to find peace. The Serenity Prayer has a lesser-known second verse: "Living one day at a time, enjoying one moment at a time, accepting hardship as a pathway to peace... ."[8] Mindfulness takes practice, patience, and time.

Doubt: Too Little Faith

Growing up without a concept of faith, I was tormented by worry. My mother kept a *Peanuts* cartoon on our refrigerator. Franklin, one of the characters, said, "I worried about this test all night.... . I got an 'A.' I wasted a good worry."[9] Worrying is a waste of time and, like anxiety, can cause physical problems. Charles Mayo, a founder of the Mayo Clinic, said, "Worry affects circulation, the heart, the glands, the whole nervous system . . . I have never known a man who died from overwork, but many who died from doubt."[10] If you had a bad interaction with a coworker on Friday, can you let it go? Or do you obsess about it all weekend?

Today, I see worry as a failure of hope and faith, thinking that I'm in control. Instead, I try to relax. Trying to control outcomes can worsen a situation and, sometimes, ensures the outcome we wanted to avoid. The employee who fears being laid off and constantly asks, "Am I on the list?" is sure to land at the top. They cause their manager time and stress—and make it easier for the manager to give them the answer they fear.

As a contact tracer, Malcolm was gripped by fear about when his job would end and then paralyzed by what to do next. His concerns are understandable: Anyone in a layoff situation would be worried about when their time is up. They have absolutely no control over the decision or timing, but they can choose how much stress to take on. In this case, Malcolm waited it out and managed his emotions as best he could. When he did get laid off, he chose to look for a new job quickly rather than apply for unemployment insurance. He was hopeful *and* took a leap of faith that he would find something and not miss too much income.

Although doubt has value, which we'll explore later in the chapter, it can make us insecure and indecisive. We don't trust our own skills and abilities, despite positive feedback and performance reviews. Hesitancy because of doubt or uncertainty can hold us back. Succumbing to our fears, we don't apply for jobs or turn down a promotion because we lack confidence in our abilities. In these situations, we need to have faith and trust that others judge our competence more accurately than we can judge our own. If we're riddled by self-doubt, we also don't inspire others' trust in us. They need us to be confident, to present ourselves as trustworthy—worthy of their trust.

Gullibility: Too Much Faith

People are prone to manipulation. Every year, phishing emails and fake websites cost people billions of dollars. What makes people susceptible to these crimes? Hackers and scammers are crafty and know how to exploit our trust. They use unethical persuasion tactics and prey on our emotions. Inventing tragic stories, creating a false sense of urgency, impersonating someone we know, offering a big return for a small investment—all these strategies leave us vulnerable to manipulation.

We're also susceptible because of our own gullibility. We don't always critically examine information we receive; we take shortcuts because of four major issues:

- Too Much Information: We can't read everything, so we apply filters, accepting information that already aligns with our beliefs and letting ourselves get drawn into what we find funny or outrageous. We scroll through a social media site and like what we see, usually posted by people we know, without too much thought.
- Not Enough Meaning: When we're confused by what we read or see, we try to make sense of it by making assumptions or oversimplifying information. We draw conclusions that may be false. Reading conflicting information can be overwhelming and requires careful attention to understand.
- Need to Act Fast: Competitive workplaces, driven by wanting to be the first or the best, often require quick decisions and actions. These market conditions don't allow enough time for reflection and critical thinking.
- Limited Memory: With so much happening so quickly, we can't remember details, so we fill in the blanks. We rely on too little information to draw sound conclusions and are prone to generalizations and stereotypes.[11]

In other words, we believe what isn't true. Taking more time and being more intentional about how we evaluate information and analyze problems improves our decisions.

In interpersonal situations, we trust—but verify. We keep our "eyes wide open" as we observe our coworkers blaming us for their mistakes or asking for yet another favor. We're gullible when we fall into a pattern of acting in ways that benefit others and harm us. As the saying goes, "Fool me once, shame on you. Fool me twice, shame on me." How many times do we need to be fooled before we begin to, appropriately, doubt?

The Narrow Ridge of Faith

When we trust but verify, we find balance. In the most challenging of times, we may, despite our doubts, fully accept and learn to live with the reality of our situation. We learn to live with uncertainty, knowing we don't have all the answers, and get comfortable with a certain amount of dependence and failure.

Acceptance

Wrongfully convicted at 20 years old of murdering her roommate, Amanda Knox walked the narrow ridge of faith. Knox was a public figure during the high-profile case, which took place while she was an exchange student in Italy. Although Knox was acquitted and released, she spent four years in an Italian prison. She reflected on an "epiphany" she had during that time:

> The conviction, the sentence, the prison cell—*this* was my life. There was no life I *should* have been living... . however small, cruel, sad, and unfair this life was, it was *my* life. Mine to make meaning out of, mine to live to the best of my ability... . whether I was eventually found innocent and freed, or not.[12]

Knox describes a deep acceptance despite her relentless sadness: "I was slowly and deliberately walking a tightrope across a bottomless foggy abyss, with no clue where I was going and nothing to hold onto but my strong, instinctual sense of balance."[13] Part of her process was to imagine different scenarios, for example, her death instead of her roommate's, her acquittal, and her suicide. She says this freed her up to focus on her current situation and to make the most of every day as best she could.

In Knox's story, we see the value of faith as acceptance of her reality. She describes her experience of walking the narrow ridge between possible outcomes and finding peace with any of them, even the worst possible scenario. Knox's process illustrates how to accept our situation even in the darkest of times.

Discomfort and Uncertainty

Struggling between doubt and faith and avoiding gullibility puts us in an uncomfortable space. We might prefer to be certain—to know that we'll be OK regardless of what happens in our career—but we can never be sure, and this uncertainty causes stress. Our "intolerance of uncertainty" causes us to want answers, just as we find quick, easy answers on our devices.[14] It may not feel good, but we learn best when we are uncomfortable.[15] Living without our addictive substance or behavior makes us uncomfortable but opens us up to new ways of thinking.

The narrow ridge is a middle, uncomfortable place. Being too comfortable, for example, in a 30-year job, might make us complacent and vulnerable. We might not see our shortcomings because we're never challenged to try new things. On the other hand, being too uncomfortable, for example, in constant fear of being yelled at or criticized, makes us defensive and reactive, unable to take risks. If our failures provoke shame and reactivity, we won't be in a conducive place to learn either. We need just enough discomfort to learn and grow.

Living with discomfort and uncertainty could mean having conflicting truths. A friend told me about the best and worst manager he ever had—the same person. The manager's priority was on my friend's development: She spent hours coaching him and put him in stretch roles to challenge him. But when he made a mistake, she was critical and accusatory, sometimes embarrassing him in front of others. Recognizing the extremes of his manager's behavior, my friend maintained a healthy skepticism about her encouragement. He could both accept her mentorship and be suspicious of her reactions.

My friend labeled his manager as "insecure." This may be true, but we learn in Twelve Step programs not to "take other people's inventory." We observe behaviors so we can navigate relationships and, if we're up to it, we share our observations. But we don't analyze motives or point out character weaknesses; that's for the other to do. We focus on our own feelings and behaviors and, when necessary, protect ourselves from harm.

Living with uncertainty is challenging. Sometimes any answer is better than no answer. We want to "move on," even if we don't get the answer we want. One way to deal with ambiguity is to do "the next right thing," as we hear in the rooms of recovery. We keep going despite feelings of doubt or despair. Amanda Knox lived her life one day at a time: reading, writing, and exercising. At work, this may look like driving to work, opening your email, changing into your uniform, or going to your next meeting. We let the day carry us. Despite the stress, work provides big advantages: scheduled activities and people relying on us. Constant busyness as a distraction could be damaging if we avoid facing real problems, but when we're stuck or depressed, activity can be an effective short-term solution.

The Paradox of Dependence

Faith is a kind of dependence. In the book *Twelve Steps and Twelve Traditions*, Bill W. describes the alcoholic's bristling at the thought of a "dependence" on a higher power. He gives the example of our dependence on electricity—not seeing it but relying on it to work, which, paradoxically, gives us more independence.[16] The same can be said of work: We depend on our employer so we can be financially independent. We depend on technology that we don't necessarily understand so we can work more efficiently. In these examples, dependence is a source of strength, not a weakness.

For teams to function well, we depend on each other's work, but we also need clear expectations. In addition to having a detailed project plan, a team contract or agreement sets standards for the quality of work and how teams communicate, for example, preferred methods and time frames for replies. A contract may also identify consequences when people don't follow agreed guidelines. These agreements reduce doubt and allow more faith among the team.

Reframing Worries

Reframing our worries increases our ability to cope.[17] We can face our fears and doubts without obsessing. Catastrophizing, or imagining the worst-case scenario even if it's unlikely to happen, is a cognitive distortion. Instead, we take a step back to assess—or reappraise—the likelihood of an outcome, and then identify ways we can cope. Amanda Knox used this strategy to imagine different outcomes she knew weren't true. Then she could free herself to accept reality.

One common stress-producing situation is public speaking. Anxious presenters imagine the worst possible outcome: being ridiculed by the audience, freezing, forgetting what they're going to say, or sweating profusely. But research shows that presenters don't appear as nervous as they feel, and simple strategies can reduce speech anxiety. Reframing nervousness as excitement, thinking of the presentation as more of a conversation, viewing stress indicators as motivation, and imagining positive reactions can increase confidence.[18] With more confidence, we have more faith that we'll do well; our doubts about ourselves and our performance subside.

Closing Thoughts

In one Twelve Step program, a reading describes the value of recovery work:

> As we make spiritual progress, we begin to feel emotion-
> ally secure. Our new attitudes bring about self-esteem, inner

strength, and serenity that is not easily shaken by any of life's hard times.[19]

We feel a sense of relief from Step Three. We learn to trust without harming ourselves and build resilience to get through hard times. We choose faith because it's an easier way to live, without the angst that would otherwise plague us.

We accept reality because we really don't have a choice. The Serenity Prayer invites us to, "accept the things I cannot change" and then offers "the courage to change the things I can,"[20] which we'll explore in the next chapter.

Reflection Questions

1. Do you consider yourself a person "of faith"? What does that mean to you?
2. What do you trust about work, your employer, or the people? How did you come to develop this trust?
3. What strategies do you have for being mindful? What practices have worked for you, and what would you like to continue, hone, or expand?
4. When have you felt doubtful at work? In retrospect, was your doubt founded? Why or why not?
5. Have you been gullible in the past? What were the signs you missed that prevented you from acting with "eyes wide open?"
6. How has faith gotten you through difficult times in a work situation?
7. What have you learned to accept at work, and how has that helped you find peace?

SECTION 2

We Come to Know Ourselves

STEP	DEFICIENCY (too little)	PRINCIPLE	EXCESS (too much)
4. Made a searching and fearless moral inventory of ourselves.	Cowardice	Courage	Recklessness
5. Admitted to God, to ourselves, and to another human being the exact nature of our wrongs.	Deceit	Integrity	Self-righteousness
6. Were entirely ready to have God remove all these defects of character.	Control	Willingness	Subservience

When we took the first three steps, we accepted external guidance. When we take the next three steps, we access a power within ourselves; we learn how to trust, and not to trust, our relationship with ourselves.

We come to know ourselves and more accurately assess who we are and who we want to become. We see how our strengths can be used for good, and we practice taking action that benefits us and others. With courage, we take a hard look at what is no longer working for us and become ready to let go of old thinking and behavior patterns. We get better at knowing what we can and can't control and practice letting go.

We try to align our jobs and our working environment with what is important to us. Because we know ourselves, we feel more grounded in making difficult decisions, taking risks, and changing in ways that support our own and the organization's goals.

CHAPTER 4

Courage

Chapter Overview

Courage means taking action for worthy goals despite the risks. We face our fears and weather the potential ambiguity, exposure, and loss to avoid cowardice. Yet we take only considered, measured risks; by assessing the possible negative consequences, we avoid recklessness, which could do more harm than good.

Courtney's Dilemma

Some work situations test our judgment and compel us to take risks despite negative personal consequences. This is a Courtney's story:

I was working for a nonprofit organization that provided computer skills training to people coming out of prison. We relied mostly on grants to fund the work, and I was responsible for the reports that told donors our success rates.

An important metric was the training completion rate—the percentage of people who finished the six-week program. My boss, the executive director, claimed that we had an 85 percent completion rate, which is pretty good compared to similar organizations' rates. But he didn't include people who dropped out of the program after the first class—about 10 percent. So, the 85 percent figure was based on people who came back to the second class.

I didn't think this was accurate, and I got up the nerve to say something to my boss. But his response was, "Well, that first class is really just an orientation." He also said, "It's not that much of a difference." But it was: 76.5 percent is the actual completion rate.

Having a job can mean a sense of community—feeling as though we belong and are part of something. Stepping out and reporting wrongdoing requires good judgment and courage because it sets us apart from others.

Courage at Work

Moral courage means taking action despite risks. We deepen our understanding of ourselves and walk through our fears, despite the complexity of a situation that may require us to act.

Action Despite Risks

The Serenity Prayer features the word courage: "God, grant me the serenity to accept the things I cannot change, courage to change the things I can, and wisdom to know the difference."[1] Change requires courage because it involves taking action despite the risks—enduring potential negative consequences to do what we believe needs to be done. Opposition comes from the outside or from within ourselves.

We're focusing on moral courage, or standing up for beliefs, principles, or values—not what we think of as physical bravery that compels firefighters and soldiers. In his book *Moral Courage*, Rushworth Kidder identifies three elements: "a commitment to moral *principles*, an awareness of the *danger* involved in supporting those principles, and a willing *endurance* of that danger."[2]

Resentments

With courage, we take Step Four and complete a "searching and fearless moral inventory of ourselves." We begin with our resentments, which eases us into the real work: identifying our role in causing harm.[3] Of course, this process is useful for work relationships. After listing everyone and everything we're angry at, we try to understand the cause and how we are affected. In other words, how are "our self-esteem, our security, our ambitions, our personal, or sex relations" negatively impacted?[4] Then, comes the tough part: What are our own mistakes or contributions to the problem? How are we "selfish, dishonest, self-seeking, and frightened?"[5] This begins a process of discovery about our character weaknesses and fears that may cause problems in our lives.

Identifying our resentments frees us up to understand the character weaknesses and fears that we may want to change. Almost everyone has some complaints about their job and, in many cases, for good reason. But a conflict with a coworker is rarely just that person's fault. We can't act with sound courage until we understand the situation from multiple perspectives.

In addition to character weaknesses, some sponsors ask us to catalog our strengths. Identifying what we believe and value gives us the fortitude to take action when appropriate. With clarity, we act on our strong principles, a good conscience, a sense of duty, or a commitment to end injustice.[6] All are worthy reasons—if we first analyzed our role.

Courage and Fear

Before recovery, we numbed our fear with addictive substances and behaviors. None of us like the fears and character weaknesses revealed when we take Step Four, but that begins our healing process. In recovery, we realize that fears are healthy human emotions; they no longer paralyze us. A Narcotics Anonymous reading reminds us, "True courage is not the absence of fear, but rather the willingness to walk through it."[7] Going to our first recovery meeting took courage. Getting through our first 24 hours without our addiction took courage.

Understanding our fears helps us prevent them from ruling our lives. Fear is typically the foundation of our character weaknesses, propping them up and protecting us, yet holding us back from developing resilience and connection. While working the steps, I realized how much of my life has been driven by fear of rejection and fear of abandonment. In some ways, these fears made me a good employee, but I was also overly compliant and rarely questioned authority for fear of being criticized. Today, when I'm resisting doing something that feels hard, I ask myself whether these fears are holding me back and how realistic they are.

For Courtney to talk to her boss took courage. Courtney had real fears and risked making her boss angry and ruining her relationship. Her boss could have yelled at her, taken responsibilities away from her, cut her out of important decisions, or fired her. Courtney could have faced even more danger if she took further action, for example, informing a news reporter about the discrepancies.

Complicated Decisions

Courtney decided not to take further action and found a new job instead. She demonstrated courage by leaving because she stayed true to her own values; quitting a job is always personally risky.

But in his book *Exit, Voice, and Loyalty*, Albert O. Hirschman argues that leaving an organization continues the cycle of bad management practices.[8] In Courtney's case, it's complicated. In a strange way, the bad data leads to more funding, which means more opportunities for people who have been incarcerated to find meaningful employment. Or, maybe industry standard is to exclude the orientation session from the data as a way of giving people an idea of what to expect before they commit to a program. Although Courtney's leaving may have continued the cycle, maybe her decision was better for the organization in the long run.

Courtney's situation is a good example of courage of an individual stepping out for a bigger goal. Many courageous acts involve standing up for others who are less willing or unable to stand up for themselves.[9] Fighting for a living wage, reporting harassment, and identifying policy inconsistencies are all examples of demonstrating courage to serve the collective rather than an individual. Courage also may include *en*couraging—supporting others as they take action.

Whistleblowers at Boeing reported safety failures long before two plane crashes killed 346 people and other problems became public. A Boeing engineer wrote in a complaint, "I was willing to stand up for safety and quality but was unable to actually have an effect in those areas," and "Boeing management was more concerned with cost and schedule than safety or quality."[10] They demonstrated courage, although their actions didn't bring about change at the time.

Not everyone can or wants to take risks associated with speaking out. If you're early in recovery or have a job for the first time in years, you might, understandably, be hesitant about taking action in certain situations. Let's explore what the extremes of courage look like and how you can decide whether or what action is appropriate.

Cowardice: Too Little Courage

Almost everything we do in recovery requires some measure of courage. American poet Maya Angelou describes the importance:

> Without courage, you cannot practice any other virtue consistently. You can be kind for a while; you can be generous for a while; you can be just for a while, or merciful for a while, even loving for a while. But it is only with courage that you can be persistently and insistently kind and generous and fair.[11]

A popular proverb is, "If you stand for nothing, you'll fall for anything." Without clear convictions—values, principles, or beliefs—we don't demonstrate courage, and we're vulnerable to others' whims. With greater clarity, which some may call their higher power, we take action despite potential consequences. In addition to standing up for others, we need courage to stand up for ourselves: to confront a coworker, to ask for a raise, and to get permission to leave work early for a recovery meeting.

These actions require difficult conversations that most people would rather avoid. We would rather text than call someone, email than meet with someone. Ghosting has become a popular, noncommunication strategy, a prime example of fleeing from instead of facing fears. In one survey, 77 percent of job candidates reported being ghosted by employers. HR managers also report being ghosted by candidates—56 percent of them after the candidate had accepted a job offer.[12] Ghosting is cowardly. It takes guts to tell an applicant they didn't get the job and to tell an employer you don't want the job. But it's the right thing to do, so the person can move on to other opportunities or candidates.

We might avoid people because we fear their judgment. Jared was asked to work late, but it was Taco Tuesday, and he didn't want to miss dinner with his family. Worried that his coworkers might tease him, he worked overtime, rationalizing the decision because of the extra pay. But it wasn't what he wanted to do. Wrapped into his fear of judgment was his own judgment of his coworkers: He assumes that they'll react in a way they might not. A common saying in Twelve Step groups is, "What other people think of me is none of my business." This is a useful mindset for disregarding others' judgments—and our own.

In a fear-based workplace culture, people are too worried to make good decisions. Mean coworkers or a punitive manager can cause employees to be paralyzed by fear and not take any action. Working environments that are de*moral*izing prevent moral action. We can see the role of despair and doubt: Why should I try to improve a situation? It's hopeless, and I have no faith that things will change. Maybe you tried to change something in the past, and nothing happened—or you were punished for trying. Of course, you feel *dis*couraged.

You also may experience burnout, or detachment, from your job. It's hard enough to do your own work, no less fight for the good of others. In these situations, you need even more courage to take positive action.

Courage means taking action despite risks, but we don't take action despite *any* risks. That's reckless, which we explore next.

Recklessness: Too Much Courage

Those of us in recovery know recklessness. Whether your "bottom" landed you in jail, in the hospital, on the streets, or just left you disconnected from yourself and your loved ones, addictive behavior is often reckless. We disregard risks and consequences and keep doing the same thing, expecting different outcomes. As we hear in recovery, this is one definition of insanity.

Let's return to Courtney's dilemma about her boss's data interpretation. If doing nothing is considered cowardly, then storming into a board of directors meeting and yelling that the executive director is unethical would be reckless—and probably ineffective.

Or maybe Courtney's concern was overblown, which could make any action seem reckless. In fact, years later, Courtney admitted to "softening" her stance on similar issues. With more experience, she noted that organizations typically "round up" success rates, and that seemed to be standard and expected. Maybe an 8.5 percent difference in completion rates wasn't significant, after all, and her decision to quit and leave an unfilled position put the organization and its clients in jeopardy. That could be considered reckless too. Sometimes, only after we act do we see more options.

Before acting, consider your motives. In recovery, many of us worked on our self-centeredness. One measure of recklessness is drawing more attention to yourself than to the issues you're railing against. Do you really want to be helpful to others, or are you acting because of your own pride, maybe wanting to be recognized? Or do you want to "save" people who don't want to be saved? Are you protecting people who don't want or need your protection? We need to be particularly careful about coercing others into following our "courageous" action. Having courage doesn't mean our way is the only way.

In addition, before we swear to "die on the sword" of a cause, we need to be certain that the cause is worth dying for. Bruce, a graphic artist, prides himself on tagging public buildings with big, colorful murals. He views his work as an act of necessary defiance, fighting against the establishment for rules he doesn't believe in. But Bruce risks getting caught, resulting in another run-in with the police and a fine he can't afford, which would put his family in jeopardy. When we're reckless, we may do more harm than good.

The Narrow Ridge of Courage

To demonstrate courage is to take *measured* risks. We need good judgment, outside perspectives, and emotional regulation to take useful, moral action. Still, whether and how to step up is complicated with no perfect path.

Risk Assessment

In his book *Moral Courage*, Rushworth Kidder identifies three risks to consider before taking courageous action: ambiguity, exposure, and loss.[13] Let's use the example of Christian Smalls, an Amazon employee who led a unionization effort at the Staten Island, NY, facility:

- Ambiguity: Deciding whether to act means looking at complex and conflicting perspectives. Situations that require courage aren't straightforward. Smalls may have had conflicted feelings about forming a union at Amazon. He had worked at the warehouse for five years and probably felt some loyalty to the company. Also, the union activity started shortly after the company introduced new benefits, which strengthened the company's position and complicated public perception.

- Exposure: Demonstrating courage means being vulnerable— exposing ourselves emotionally. Amazon's general counsel wrote about Smalls, which got leaked to the press: "He's not smart, or articulate."[14] Stepping out during a controversial situation often results in public scrutiny, which can be embarrassing.

- Loss: Taking courageous action may result in losing our reputation, our relationships, our job, and more. Smalls was fired from his job. Amazon executives claimed that he violated a quarantine order during the COVID-19 pandemic, but Smalls believes it was because of his activism.[15] Union organizers may be ostracized by coworkers who don't agree with them. They also risk losing wages if they strike.

In the end, we decide whether taking action is worth the risk. To find balance along the narrow ridge, we ask whether the rewards outweigh the ambiguity, exposure, and loss.

Outside Perspectives

As for all difficult work situations, there is no one perfect response. Mirabelle, an assistant at a day care center, overheard another assistant say to a child, "I'm going to slap you if you don't cut it out." Two other employees also heard the comment. They got together and talked about what to do, and they agreed: Mirabelle would report the assistant. She did, and the woman was fired. As Mirabelle says, "It was for the best. It obviously wasn't the right job for her."

Other situations are more nuanced. If Mirabelle was the only one who heard the comment and it wasn't clear whether the assistant was joking, Mirabelle would be in a tougher spot. She could consult a coworker or her supervisor for suggestions. In active addiction, her thinking was extreme, so now she doesn't want to be too heavy handed —or too dismissive.

When Kim Gwang-ho reported safety issues at Hyundai, he first checked with his wife, who was worried about the financial consequences.[16] Eventually, he convinced her, but she was involved in his decision process.

Assessing risks means preparing for all possible outcomes. People close to the situation and detached from the situation help us work through different scenarios. What if we are ignored, ridiculed, gaslit, or yelled at? What if we are escorted off the premises or fired on the spot? What if the message is immediately well received—maybe too easily accepted? Knowing what we might face helps us prepare for the worst, while we hope, and prepare, for the best.

Emotional Regulation

In addition to deciding *whether* to act courageously, we choose *how* we take action. Once the decision is made, courageous people act with confidence—with "integrity and intention,"[17] knowing we're doing the right thing and having a clear goal in mind. Courtney prepared for a difficult conversation with her executive director about the data reporting. She couldn't sound too wishy-washy, or her boss wouldn't take her concerns seriously. But sounding too brash might seem threatening and could damage trust, putting the director on the defense.

When Mirabelle reported the caregiver, she prepared to be uncomfortable but wasn't undone by her discomfort. In recovery, she knows that discomfort is a sign of growth, and she welcomed the opportunity.

With a direct approach, she described what she observed. She knew what was right, so she was calm and firm, not strident and accusatory.

In both cases and others that require courage, emotional regulation is critical. We don't deny our emotions and visceral reactions; they serve as important signals about what could be wrong, what we feel is intolerable, and how we might respond. As despair lurks in the background, we call on hope. We remember situations we handled well in the past, rely on our support network, and act with courage.

Closing Thoughts

Courageous action requires a measured, thoughtful approach. In situations that demand our attention, we use skills we learned in recovery—assessing our character weaknesses, walking through our fears, talking with others to get outside perspectives, and assessing risk before taking action.

AA literature explains courage: "Prudence means taking calculated chances ... . Readiness to take consequences of our past and to take responsibility for [the] well-being of others."[18] One of the many gifts of sobriety is a clear head. In work situations that demand courage, we're up to the task, as long as we use that clear head to make rational decisions.

Reflection Questions

1. Who in your life do you consider to be courageous? In what ways does this person demonstrate courage? What risks do they take, and what outcomes do they achieve?

2. Think about a time when you challenged a policy, practice, or something else you thought was unethical at work. What skills did you use? What did you accomplish?

3. Describe a time when you made an unpopular decision at work. How did you demonstrate courage in that situation?

4. Describe a time when you didn't speak up about something you thought was important. What made it not worth fighting for, or what held you back? What can you learn from the experience?

5. Were you ever reckless at work? What risks did you fail to recognize? How can you identify similar risks in the future?

6. Think about a time when you encouraged others to follow your idea or recommendation. How were you successful in getting people to adopt your perspective? How did others respond?

CHAPTER 5

Integrity

Chapter Overview

During our fifth step in recovery, we reveal our secrets and face our past. This process can make us feel whole—fully integrated—and allow us to live by our values. To become people of integrity, we practiced authenticity and consistency and avoided deceiving others or being rigid and self-righteous. Over time, we became more trustworthy despite the complexity of conflicting values and other complications of work.

Anthony's Dilemma

Sometimes we do jobs that don't align with our values. Here's Anthony's story:

I found what seemed like the perfect job, working as a career coach for a small job placement company. I was coaching people who had been laid off or were changing careers to help them identify their strengths, clarify their goals, prepare their resume and cover letters, and land new positions.

But from the start, I ignored some signs because I needed the work. The company name included an Ivy League university name and color, without any affiliation to the school. It looked fake.

After a few months, I saw more of the sales side of the business. The owner used manipulative tactics to get people to pay thousands of dollars for the service. When I sat in on a meeting, I saw that he would make "prospects" feel terrible, as though they could never get a job on their own without our help. It was painful to watch! He also said we had personal connections with employers that we didn't have.

Anthony knew better, and he eventually made the right decision for himself. He got clarity about what was important to him and how he wanted to live his values. He acted with integrity.

Integrity at Work

From a word meaning whole, integrity means being real, consistent, and principled, or values driven. When we have integrity, we're our genuine selves at work and do what we say we'll do. We establish our credibility and people choose to trust us.

Honest and Whole

People who have integrity are honest and whole—acting consistently according to who they are and what they believe. You may agree with these statements for yourself, which indicate integrity:

- It is more important to be myself than to be popular.
- When people keep telling the truth, things work out.
- I would never lie just to get something I wanted from someone.
- My life is guided and given meaning by my code of values.
- It is important to me to be open and honest about my feelings.
- I always follow through on my commitments, even when it costs me.
- I dislike phonies who pretend to be what they are not.[1]

In these statements, we see connections to other program principles. Honesty—telling the truth and not lying—is a part of integrity, but integrity is broader. The root of the word is integer, meaning whole or intact.[2] Integrity means not only telling the truth but also being real, consistent, and values driven. We see the importance of integrity for courage. Putting popularity and personal costs second are hallmarks of taking courageous action.

When we move from Step Four to Step Five in a Twelve Step program, we say our inventory out loud to another person, typically a sponsor. As we hear in the rooms of recovery, "We're as sick as our secrets." After years of shame, we speak our truth and feel relief from the retelling. We begin to feel whole, or integral, again, making sense of our lives—who we were, who we are now, and who we may become in the future.

Authenticity

Being authentic means acting as our true selves. How we express ourselves is consistent with how we think and feel about ourselves, including our values and identities.[3] We present ourselves as we truly are: imperfect and whole. What we gain from revealing ourselves during Step Five is practicing being vulnerable, and it pays off. People who are authentic are happier and have better relationships than people who are inauthentic, who experience more depression and anxiety.[4]

Some of us with addiction histories felt as though we never belonged. We twisted ourselves into knots trying to fit in, or we decided we were "terminally unique," as I've heard in recovery. This kept us apart in our personal and professional lives, believing we were either better or worse than everyone else—or just so different that no one could possibly understand us. For some of us, this was the reason we gave for our addictive behavior.

But, as it turns out, people want to work with people who are genuine and who share more about themselves.[5] Coworkers might accept us if we give them a chance. In the chapter on honesty, you read about an Intel employee who revealed his addiction history. He may feel as though his recovery is an integral part of who he is. People who share more of themselves at work report liking their jobs more, feeling less stress, and feeling more engaged and connected with others.[6]

Consistency and Credibility

At its core, integrity is about consistency. People assess whether we have integrity by our behaviors. Do we keep our promises? Do we do what we say we'll do? Researchers call this behavioral integrity: matching our actions to our words.[7]

But having behavioral consistency isn't enough to be considered a person of high integrity. A leader can be a consistent jerk. We also must live by moral standards. Do we "walk the talk" and "practice what we preach"? Do we prioritize the same things we say are important?

Unfortunately, this disconnect is common in organizations. A company that spouts "putting customers first" and then routinely denies warranty coverage is inconsistent—not living up to its own standards and what customers expect. Companies often have codes of conduct written on walls and in handbooks that employees sign, but they aren't consistently applied or followed.

Sometimes, people in organizations answer to their own moral principles, or a higher power, as discussed earlier. People with integrity act ethically for themselves, not for public approval. Their values supersede company codes.

Like integrity, credibility is demonstrated over time. At work, we want to be perceived as credible, meaning what we say is reliable and believable. We become credible by first trusting our own experience, education, and expertise; then, we can be trusted by others.

Watch any *Shark Tank* episode and you'll see the investors ask the entrepreneur about their background. As the entrepreneur describes their experience as well as their own story and motivation for developing the product, sharks decide whether they have credibility to run a successful business. In some cases, entrepreneurs ask for too much money and lose credibility with the sharks. What they say isn't reliable, and the sharks feel deceived.

Deceit: Too Little Integrity

Just as the job placement company deceived clients, Anthony deceived himself. He saw the company logo when he applied for the job, with its knockoff name and color. Because the job was in his field and paid well, he convinced himself that his work was clean.

To be rigorously honest, we evaluate our own contribution to a larger system—a whole, integral system that is complete only with our participation. Purdue Pharma faced more than $1 trillion in claims about deceptive sales and marketing practices that led to the opioid epidemic. The Sackler family, who managed the company, didn't act alone. Sales reps who pushed these addictive drugs received generous compensation, and doctors who prescribed the drugs accepted paid speaking engagements and trips. Many stakeholders in these companies had a role in making the system run.

We're complicit in deception when we act in ways that don't feel right to us. Cognitive dissonance is a sign of inconsistency and possibly deceit. We feel this psychological tension when our actions contradict our values and beliefs. When doctors recognized that patients were becoming addicted to opioids even when taking the medication as prescribed, they likely experienced cognitive dissonance. Then they faced a contradiction between their commitment to healing people and their prescribing harmful drugs. Cognitive dissonance is a helpful signal that we aren't acting with integrity.

If consistency is essential to integrity, then inconsistency could be a sign of deceit. At a personal level, it's easy to spot someone who seems "fake." They might act like a chameleon, changing their personality when they interact with different people. Or they might seem plastic or stiff, as though their clothes don't quite fit or they're uncomfortable in their own skin. Or they might seem evasive, avoiding questions or choosing their words a little too carefully. You may feel as though they are flattering you or trying too hard to be liked. Images fill social media pages to present a curated image of someone we may never really know.

Gossip or talking behind someone's back is another example of deceit. When we say or act one way with people to their face but criticize them to others, we're being inconsistent. Bill W. warns that gossip is satisfying and makes us feel superior. He describes it as "self-righteous anger,"[8] which we'll explore next.

Self-Righteousness: Too Much Integrity

Integrity bleeds over to self-righteousness when we feel morally superior to others. How can we be sure that our truth is the only truth? Some of us in recovery know self-righteousness well. Once we got sober, we harshly judged others who were still drinking or using. Then we learned that everyone has their own path.

As we do before taking courageous action, we seek outside opinions to check our intuition before taking radical action in the name of integrity. We check what's right for us *and* what's right for others. Getting other perspectives avoids relying on only our own sense of right and wrong.

Embedded in self-righteousness may be a level of anger and frustration we tried to shed in recovery. We may be so blinded by our own judgment and others' failure to measure up to our rigid moral standards that it's maddening. It's interesting to think about having a high tolerance for an addictive substance but so little tolerance in other areas of our lives.

Authenticity also isn't an excuse for being insensitive. We're too rigid if we proclaim, "I can't change who I am" or "This is just who I am" when we really mean, "I don't care about others' views or feelings." Upholding our own values so strongly that we lose empathy for others is self-righteousness.

One danger of self-righteousness is hypocrisy. If our professed values are so high and so rigid that even we can't possibly live up to them, we may be perceived as hypocritical. Again, we say one thing but do another. This happens—we're not perfect. But we acknowledge contradictions openly and learn from them.

Integrity also might run amok when authenticity is performative. We talk about our addiction histories and all that we've suffered and wear it as a badge. Online or in person, we curate an image of "who we really are." While this image typically puts people in a positive light, some of us in recovery paint an image that exaggerates our warts. We put our troubled past on display and let it define us. But in the end, it's still a fake persona that keeps us stuck where we are.

The Narrow Ridge of Integrity

Integrity might seem easy, but it's impossible to achieve perfectly. Conflicting values and work requirements cause us to make difficult choices. Although, overall, we are authentic, we do act differently depending on the situation. Transparency is one way to walk the narrow ridge: We don't intentionally withhold important information or confuse people.

Conflicting Values

We run into trouble when we try to do the right thing but face conflicting values. Maggie, a psychiatric nurse, had a patient who refused medication that helped manage violent behavior that threatened the safety of others. How does she balance the patient's autonomy—the right to refuse medication—and the rights of other patients to a safe environment? Both are core values of the hospital. In this case, Maggie could be deceitful, for example, by manipulating the patient into taking medication or by not telling other patients about the potential harm. Or she could be self-righteous, for example, stridently protecting the patient's autonomy or exaggerating the risks to other patients.

These situations have no easy answers. Others must be consulted to find a solution that isn't ideal but that balances, in a complex, ethical situation like this, patient rights, patient safety, organizational standards, federal or state guidelines, legal regulations—and Maggie's own values and beliefs.

At other times, the conflicting values are between ourselves and where we work. An environmentalist might take a job that damages the environment, or a former smoker might work at a tobacco company. Particularly for people who are recently coming out of addiction, job opportunities may be limited. Focusing on the good work we do within our job responsibilities or volunteering outside of work can help counteract our daily work.

Conflicting values also may be within ourselves. Working at a salt mine, Nate didn't like contributing to environmental damage, but he did value having a secure, well-paying job for people who depended on him. He also valued the people he worked with; they were like family, and they looked after each other. No job is perfect.

Self-Presentation

Being authentic implies consistency but not a fixed state. We're adaptable in situations, as mentioned earlier, and no one is exactly the same with everyone in their life. You're different with your spouse, a coworker who is a friend, a customer, and your child. At times, we may need to hide aspects of ourselves at work. Not all work environments are safe for people who, for example, are in a same-sex relationship or practice a particular religion. In recovery, we learn how to protect ourselves in healthy ways.

Good judgment guides decisions about what to reveal and what to keep to yourself. We know the benefits of being our true selves at work, but this isn't possible or practical for everyone. Companies talk about hiring for "organizational fit." It's also OK if your job isn't a fit for *you*. If you can change jobs to be in a place that's more accepting, great; if not, that's an unfortunate reality, right now, that you may hope will change in the future.

We also change over time. In recovery, we may be discovering who we really are for the first time. In new jobs, we experiment with different attire, interpersonal approaches, and communication styles to see what works best given the environment.[9] That's how we adapt and grow.

Transparency

Transparent communication helps us along the narrow ridge. Whatever decision Maggie makes about her patient, she should be fully transparent, meaning she discloses information clearly and accurately. This is complicated by laws that protect both patient privacy and patient safety. But if the patient is off medication and is a danger to others, they have a right to know if they are at risk. When we consider disclosing information that may be confidential, we weigh personal rights with the potential impact on others.

One check of our integrity is how we would feel if our decision were made public. If Maggie's sponsor or a family member found out, would she still stand by her choice? If a newspaper article described the situation and her actions, would she feel embarrassed or OK?

When we communicate, our language, within reason, should be simple. Some jargon that's relevant within our workgroup, profession, or industry is necessary. But when fancy language is used to intentionally confuse or embarrass people, they may question our integrity. We may complicate what we say for selfish purposes. A computer technician wants to show how hard her job is, or a house contractor wants to exclude a homeowner from decisions. It's worth asking yourself whether your language is appropriate for the audience. Does the person understand what you're saying? Is the information useful?

Transparency could involve committing publicly to action. Before we can walk the talk, we need the talk. Oaths to public office allow us to hold our leaders accountable—somewhat. People are more likely to keep their commitments if they're made publicly, which is why we make our New Year's resolutions known.[10] When you volunteer for a work function, your coworkers expect you to show up.

Yet we can't be expected to keep all our commitments. Things happen: People get sick and make mistakes. If we were untrustworthy in active addiction, people may need time to recognize and trust the changes we've made. But if we typically do what we say we'll do and act in sync with our values, people will, over time, come to view us as having integrity.

Closing Thoughts

"To Thine Own Self Be True" appears on the backs of many Twelve Step medallions. The quote from Shakespeare's *Hamlet* continues, "And it must follow, as the night the day, Thou canst not then be false to any man." Although the original meaning was probably more about benefiting ourselves first,[11] an AA member used the phrase in a talk, "Honesty with One's Self." He explained, "Sincerity means the difference between those who accomplish their aims in AA and those who don't."[12]

Today, we may interpret this as knowing ourselves, doing what's right, and following through on our commitments. We are true to ourselves and true to others. It takes consistency to be trustworthy. We can slip from time to time but not too much. People with integrity are depended upon and become leaders in organizations.

Reflection Questions

1. Describe someone you know who has integrity. How have they gained your respect?
2. What values do you consider most important in your work life?[13]
3. Describe a time when you felt most like yourself during your career. How can you replicate that time today?
4. How well do you keep your commitments? What would inspire people to rely on you more?
5. Were you self-righteous about something at work? What caused you to hold the position so strongly? What was the impact on your relationships? What would you do differently if you faced a similar situation?
6. When have you made a difficult decision that involved conflicting values or truths? How did you reveal your decision to others? What did you learn from the experience?

CHAPTER 6

Willingness

Chapter Overview

For some of us, in the extremes of our addiction, we felt either completely in control or entirely out of control. Willingness means letting go of what no longer works for us and others, knowing that our strengths and weaknesses are two sides of the same coin. Although we choose to surrender, we aren't subservient. We get comfortable in middle spaces, particularly during times of personal and organizational change.

Alex's Dilemma

Once again, the steps gently guide us into action. Before we let go of anything, we're asked to find the willingness, which Alex resisted. Here's her story:

Lydia and I worked together for 14 years. As my assistant, she ordered supplies and, most important, was the first line of defense in the office when people dropped by. I completely relied on her to protect me from interruptions during the day.

A vice president said assistants needed to be "upskilled," so Lydia was moved to another position, and I was given a different assistant. At first, I was devastated. I couldn't imagine working with anyone else.

Six months later, I understand the decision. My new assistant has spreadsheet and organizational skills that make me much more productive. He manages the influx of people, but that's a small part of what he does to support my work.

I realized that I was holding on to Lydia out of fear and self-centeredness. Once I let go, I saw the benefits, but it was a painful process getting there.

Willingness, or being open, is the first step to change. Without it, we hold fast to our past and stay stuck. In Step Three, we addressed an existential willingness, which led us to faith. In Step Six, we become willing to make changes ourselves.

Willingness at Work

In Step Six, we're asked to be "ready" for change. We become willing to let go of old patterns and behaviors that protected us in the past but no longer serve us or others. After we admit our shortcomings, willingness becomes the driver toward action.

Old Patterns

A favorite saying in Twelve Step programs is, "My best thinking got me here," meaning old ways of thinking haven't exactly worked out well for us, and it's time for a change. My obsession with email has plagued me in every job. My thinking was based on irrational fear: that if I didn't respond quickly to email, then I was dispensable. Constantly checking and answering email interrupted time with family and friends. We all hold beliefs that guide our patterns of behavior; some are functional, but mine was not.

In his speech at a 1976 AA convention, Sandy B. joked, "All you have to do is … don't drink, turn your life over to God, and get rid of all of your old ideas. That's *all* we ask. That's *all* we ask that you do." Then Sandy compares his ideas to "carrying around a 150-pound rock. But it was my rock. It was mine. I put this thing together. This was the real me!"[1] Sandy B.'s speech is hilarious and was reimagined in a popular book, *Drop the Rock*. In the book, Mary is trying to swim to a boat, but she's carrying her rock of "resentments, fear, dishonesty, self-pity, intolerance, and anger."[2] People yell, "Mary, drop the rock! Let go and drop the rock," which she finally does and easily swims to the boat.[3]

In active addiction, we do anything to hang on. We blame others for our problems as a way to rationalize our character weaknesses and deny our own role. Only when our past ways of being become too painful—sometimes literally dragging us down—are we ready for change. In other words, even though change is difficult, it's easier than holding on to a big rock.

Willingness as the Key

Bill W. described willingness as the key to unlocking the door that leads to faith,[4] which is why willingness is often associated with Step Three. But Step Six requires a more practical willingness. When we're willing, we're ready to give up behaviors and thought patterns that no longer serve us or others. Jeff was the fun one at work and could easily gather a crowd in the breakroom. But his jokes were biting and sarcastic, often at others' expense. In recovery, he realized that he played this role because he needed to be liked and was afraid of feeling left out. This awareness let him imagine a different way of being—the beginning of change and a willingness to benefit instead of disparage others.

At some point in recovery, we stop fighting, recognizing that resisting only makes change more difficult. Pushing against intrusive thoughts can intensify them, which can reinforce old thought patterns. For example, the more we focus on *not* engaging in addictive behavior, the more we may want to. In meditation practices, which we'll explore later, we observe our thoughts but let them float by.

Willingness is about being open, being receptive. We don't know what may come until we have patience to allow and receive it. Alex held so tightly to Lydia that she prevented her from developing new skills. Lydia was trained to work well for her but *only* for her; she lacked baseline skills required for the job. In contrast, Jim, a manager in another department, focused on his assistant's development. He saw his role as expanding others' skills and helping them to move on.

In a sense, willingness is surrendering, which has negative connotations. When we think of surrendering, we might think of situations with devastating consequences, for example, war or cancer. Although it seems like a loss of power, surrendering is a powerful act. The authors of *Drop the Rock* explain, "Not a passive, waiting surrender, but an active use of the will; a total surrender of mind (thinking) and body (doing)."[5] We take action for a greater good—for a better future for ourselves or others. Then, we can live in a state of wonder ("I wonder what will happen") and experience peace.

Letting Go

An abundance of religious and nonreligious sayings encourage us to "Let it go," "Let go and let God," "Turn it over," "Leave it in God's hands," "Let the chips fall where they may," "Roll with the punches," and "Go with the flow." Sayings remind us that "It is what it is," "This too shall pass," "Maybe it's not meant to be," "Thy will be done," "Whatever will be, will be" ("Que sera sera"), "That's life" ("C'est la vie"), and "Time will tell."

Some of us want to fix everything. Lessons from Al-Anon for families and friends of alcoholics teach Three Cs: "I didn't cause it, I can't control it, and I can't cure it."[6] Even if we lead a team—and maybe particularly if we lead a team—we need to let people contribute in their own way. The leader doesn't have to lead every meeting or proofread every deck. Leading means identifying others' strengths and letting people use those strengths.

Another useful strategy is "Let them."[7] Let people do what they need to do without our interference or the stress of trying to control them, particularly if it doesn't affect us. Your company implements yet another app to "improve collaboration"? Let them. Your coworker brags to your manager? Let him. Your client wants to get three more bids for the job, let her. In recovery, we have friends who have relapsed and, unfortunately, we learn that "let them" is sometimes our only choice. We can apply that same approach to people at work.

The story about dropping the rock is about literally letting go. Surrendering can feel like a physical act that allows our bodies to relax. When Mary dropped the rock, gravity did the rest. When we take Step Six, some of us practice a ritual for letting go. We write fears on a piece of paper and burn it, create a God box to hold our character weaknesses, or carry a worry stone to remind us of a weight we're holding onto. At work, we might organize our workspace to get rid of the clutter, buy new clothes to set a new intention, or complete an annual self-review to identify changes we'll implement next year.

Control: Too Little Willingness

So much at work is out of our control. For most of us, we don't control our work hours or assignments. Even if we own a business, we can't possibly control all outcomes. At a minimum, we rely on others to buy our services and supply our products, and most of us work as part of an interdependent team. Given these constraints, we might try to grab control where we can.

Our biggest temptation is to try to control people we work with. Feeling out of control ourselves, we might want others to submit to what we want, how we want them to be. Being self-centered and judgmental, we don't know or don't care what path is best for them; we know best. We do this for selfish reasons: to reduce our fear and make ourselves feel better. Micromanagers inspect every detail because of their own fears: fear of not measuring up, fear of being criticized, or fear of losing their job.

Overfunctioning is another way we try to maintain control. Distrusting others, Brandon, a software engineer, didn't give others a chance to contribute. During project planning, he took on all the important tasks, and then swooped in before others could do theirs. He withheld information, so people couldn't do their part even if they wanted to. Then he complained that he did all the work and no one else stepped up. Brandon needed to trust his teammates to succeed—or to fail. Either way, people need leeway to learn and make mistakes. People don't grow in organizations unless they're given room to fail.

As employees, we want some autonomy—not to be controlled but to have more control over our own work. We have intrinsic motivation and want to make our own decisions. We want flexibility to choose, for example, when we work at home or at the office. Having control over what and how we do our work improves job satisfaction.[8] Leaders should consider writing guidelines instead of policies and giving suggestions instead of directions. Strict measures of control lead to compliance but stifle adaptability and innovation. Employees can contribute more than simply following along. They can be trusted to make good, ethical choices, if we let them.[9]

People with addiction histories know control. We tried to control our drinking or using and couldn't. But one theory is that addiction is not about a lack of control but about an obsession with it. We drink to try to control what seems uncontrollable; we drink to feel normal. We self-medicate after (or before or during) work because we can't deal with things the way they are.[10] Recovery teaches us to release our tight grip, allowing space for better things to come.

Subservience: Too Much Willingness

Just as gullibility makes us vulnerable to deception, subservience leaves us vulnerable to mistreatment. When we're subservient, we give up personal power and control but not in a healthy way. We do so reflexively, without thinking, unlike when we consciously choose to surrender. We have no autonomy at all and allow, or somehow even prefer, to be exploited.

Thankfully, language in organizations has evolved so that we no longer refer to managers as "superiors." The corporate hierarchy is unavoidable, but superior implies that someone is inferior, perhaps in more ways than in a box on an organization chart. Good leaders don't want people who are obedient; they want people who are competent, who question and find better ways of working.

Some examples of subservience are obvious. To acquiesce to sexual demands or work in unsafe conditions because of job threats is to comply and harm ourselves. Of course, people in these situations often have no choice. With varying degrees of success, we have laws to protect us.

A less obvious example of too much deference to authority is doing work we believe is unproductive. In recovery, we use our tools to figure out whether and how to say no. We analyze our resentments, determine our role, and get perspective. We ask a bunch of questions. What is the impact on me and on others? How am I contributing to the situation? What is my intuition about the situation? What does my higher power say? What would others in this situation do? What does my HR or union representative say? What are the relevant company policies?

Sometimes, we take on extra tasks for good reasons. We may want to be of service, or we have expertise to share, or we want to learn new things. Often, taking on responsibilities outside a job description sets us up for promotion.

But at what point are we being taken advantage of? Do you take on more of your share and put your health or work-life balance at risk? Could you ask that less-desirable tasks be shared more equitably? Could you ask to be rewarded in some way for your work? Or do you work in fear of being reprimanded for minor mistakes or for nothing at all? No one deserves to work in a toxic work environment that operates on subservience.

The Narrow Ridge of Willingness

Allowing willingness is a paradox like many we discuss in this book. We're neither in nor out of control, as we felt while in active addiction. We're someplace different: finding ways to accept ourselves as we are, yet being open to change.

Shadow Sides

As we consider changing our thought and behavior patterns, we acknowledge the strengths that have served us well. Katrina's competitive spirit drove her to pursue an advanced degree in a specialized field. Carter's work ethic made him a tough manager who demanded and got the very best from his staff. But every strength, when overused, has a shadow side that is a weakness. Katrina was so competitive that she compared her accomplishments to those of her coworkers, and they got tired of hearing it. Carter was so demanding that he had high turnover because people didn't want to work at his pace.

Bill George, author of *True North*, encourages us to embrace both sides of our character: "By accepting both your light and your shadow, you can become a more integrated human being who can consciously choose the middle ground between these poles."[11] This is the narrow ridge of our strengths and weaknesses. Sometimes a strength is a weakness, and sometimes a weakness is a strength.

Let's say you're both creative and a procrastinator. While you're procrastinating, you're thinking up more and more ideas. Your challenge may be in getting started and trusting that you can choose one idea and access your talent. Or, maybe you're both analytical and indecisive. Your indecision could be a by-product of looking at all sides of a complex situation. Then, your challenge is in knowing when you have gathered enough information to make a decision you can stand by. In other words, how can you avoid overusing a quality to the point that it becomes unhelpful? Although there's no exact point, can you sense when an asset becomes a liability and take that opportunity to change?

Imagine that you're asked during a job interview, "What's your greatest weakness?" Conventional advice is to turn a negative into a positive. This works best if you're honest and reflective, focusing on the value to the organization. For example, a candidate might say, "I never miss a deadline, which is usually great, but sometimes I think I could do a better job if I spend a little more time. I like to get things done and off my plate. Recently, I've been starting projects earlier to give myself more time and still not miss the deadline." Or, as someone in recovery, you may say, "I've been pretty self-centered in my life and tend to think of how things affect me first. I've been working on seeing the bigger picture to consider how my decisions impact other people." Then you might give a work example to illustrate what you do differently now.

"Act as If"

In recovery, we're advised to "act as if," to be willing to change. In psychology, this means reflecting on how we want to be different and acting "as if" we had those qualities.[12] We banish old, negative thinking about ourselves, for example, "I'm never going to do this right, so why bother?" Instead, we imagine how our lives could be better and move toward behaviors to get us there.

Another expression of this willingness is to "fake it until we make it," although that doesn't mean lying or being inauthentic. Better phrasing might be "fake it until you become it."[13] That transitional time is a narrow ridge—not being one or the other—reliable or unreliable, or organized or disorganized. On the ridge, we make a choice even though we're not quite there. We tell ourselves, "I'm going to imagine I'm a competent person who can get this done." We try out that persona and practice being that person—someone who is confident, skilled, and efficient—to see what is possible and what could eventually become second nature.

Simple physical changes could change how we feel and how we appear to those around us. Smiling may improve your mood, while scowling or frowning may make you feel more serious.[14] Although the evidence is mixed, "power poses" might help you feel more confident. When you prepare for an important event, hold a "victory pose" with your arms lifted and your chin up, or a "Wonder Woman pose" with your legs apart and your hands on your hips.[15] These expansive poses, particularly compared to contracted poses, for example, being hunched over and appearing closed and smaller,[16] may signal your mind and communicate to others that you are competent and confident.

Change Management

Like personal change, organizational change is often met with resistance. For employees to be willing to change to a new system, a new process, or new job responsibilities, leaders and teammates must understand employees' uncertainty. Employees may be afraid of not having the right skills, losing autonomy, or losing their job. This is another situation when uncertainty is a middle space—between what is and what will be—and not knowing exactly how things will turn out.

As employees, we react to change differently. At one extreme, we actively resist, taking action to sabotage the change and prevent it from happening. At the other extreme, we actively support the change, encouraging others to get on board. Or we may be somewhere in between, for example, doing the bare minimum or following along but with a bad attitude.[17] Or we may act in contradictory ways. When my former company announced a second companywide reorganization within two years, Annabelle, a marketing manager, was both angry and excited. She didn't want to move offices yet again, but she took the opportunity to carve out a new part-time job so she could spend more time with her family.

Of course, leaders want employees to support change. To reduce resistance, leaders increase communication to let employees know what to expect and to create a sense of community, which increases buy-in among a team.[18] They do this by planning the communication well in advance, by involving everyone in decisions as much as possible, by explaining the benefits, by making sure employees have the skills they need, and by listening and responding to employees' concerns as change is implemented.[19] This approach increases employees' readiness, or willingness, to change.

For employees to more willingly accept organizational changes, they can use similar strategies as those for developing faith. Checking our fears and worries to accurately assess possible outcomes can reduce uncertainties. On the other hand, as always, our fears may be real. Often, organizational changes do turn out badly for employees, and resistance may be important to improve the situation for yourself and others, as we discussed in the chapters on courage and integrity.

Having resisted personal change for so long during active addiction, some of us find ourselves in uncomfortable places during times of change at work. Should we go along? Should we be leaders and role models? Should we fight? Should we drag our feet? As we've learned in recovery, resistance just for the sake of resistance is unlikely to prevent the outcomes we dread. Instead, we ask what is best for us and best for others in the long run and make a conscious choice.

Closing Thoughts

In Step Three, we found faith, and in Step Six, we became ready for change. For both, we relinquished some control and relaxed, and we do it over and over.

Kevin Griffin, author of *One Breath at a Time: Buddhism and the Twelve Steps*, refers to letting go as "the central issue of sobriety and all spiritual growth."[20] Each time we let go, we make more space for a better version of ourselves.

When we surrender, we don't give *up* as much as we allow ourselves to give *in* and accept reality[21]—to stop fighting with ourselves, with others, and with all that we can never control.

Reflection Questions

1. What fears or resentments have you held onto? Up to what point were they helpful motivations for positive action? When did they become unhelpful or harmful? What did you notice about the shift, and what did you do?

2. Now think about unhelpful thought or behavior patterns you seem to repeat related to work or your career. How were these helpful to you in the past? In what ways do these no longer serve you or others, particularly at work? What would you need to do to change those thoughts and behaviors? What would it look like to let these go?

3. In what ways do you try to control people at work? What has been the result? How can you focus on your own reactions instead?

4. In what work situations do you feel subservient? How could you assert some authority over the situation?

5. What is both a strength and a weakness of yours? In what ways does the quality serve you and others, and in what ways does it not? How can you find balance, for example, by not overusing it and causing harm?

6. What is your default way of reacting to change? Are you more of a supporter or resister? How could you move to being more supportive when the outcome is inevitable?

SECTION 3

We Focus on Interpersonal Relationships

STEP	DEFICIENCY (too little)	PRINCIPLE	EXCESS (too much)
7. Humbly asked Him to remove our shortcomings.	Arrogance	Humility	Worthlessness
8. Made a list of all persons we had harmed, and became willing to make amends to them all.	Apathy	Compassion	Agony
9. Made direct amends to such people wherever possible, except when to do so would injure them or others.	Irresponsibility	Accountability	Manipulation

In this section, we focus on our interpersonal relationships. Steps Seven, Eight, and Nine guide us through acknowledging and addressing our shortcomings and apologizing for our failings.

At work, humility requires us to know our place within an organizational structure and to rightsize ourselves and make space for others. With compassion, we notice when others are struggling, including those we have harmed, and we take action to relieve their pain and suffering. As accountable employees, we do our best work and take initiative to solve problems.

We become more responsible people who prioritize our interactions and our care for others. Although conversations may be difficult, we don't shy away from them. Our goal is to release ourselves and others from anger, resentments, and assumptions that get in the way of more direct, positive, and productive relationships.

CHAPTER 7

Humility

Chapter Overview

Possibly the most important principle in a Twelve Step program, humility means keeping ourselves in perspective, recognizing our limitations, and making space for others. We avoid being arrogant and feeling worthless and strive for a level of confidence that helps us get what we need at work without overshadowing others.

Leah's Dilemma

Starting a new job is difficult for anyone. We balance coming across as a "know-it-all" with feeling stupid for not learning quickly enough. Here's Leah's story:

> I was really excited about being an intake coordinator at a hospital behavioral health unit. I thought the job would be easy, but there was a lot to learn. I got a three-inch manual to study about the programs, systems, and what to ask people when they call in for help.
>
> I was only a few weeks clean, so my brain was still working slowly, and I felt like I wasn't learning fast enough. I felt incompetent and couldn't keep track of everything—like I should be the one calling in for help.
>
> After a couple of weeks, I felt so stressed that I relapsed and started drinking again. Fortunately, I stopped after a few days and stuck with the job.
>
> My boss and coworkers were great. This wasn't about them. They were patient and supportive and encouraged me to ask anything. They said, "We're here for you." The funny thing is, for

all my stress, I got great feedback. One of my coworkers said that I was one of the fastest learners they had!

I did get some feedback about better questions to ask when a call comes in, and once I took down a number wrong. My boss said it happens to everyone. If they all weren't so nice, I wouldn't have lasted in that job.

All organizations are hierarchical, with more power at the top. Wherever our place in that structure, we demonstrate humility to get along within the system. Leah is finding her way early on.

Humility at Work

Being humble means having an accurate picture of ourselves—neither above nor below others. We are willing to learn, temper ourselves, and make space for others to thrive.

Rightsizing Ourselves

Humility is the core principle of Step Seven, when we "Humbly asked God to remove our shortcomings." A common saying in Twelve Step programs is, "Humility is not thinking less of yourself; it is thinking of yourself less."[1] When we're humble, we acknowledge our strengths as well as our limitations, which we learned during our fourth-step inventory.

Humility also means putting yourself in perspective or "rightsizing" yourself. After spending much of our lives mired in self-centered addiction, we work on interpersonal relationships: how we get along with others and how we compare, or don't compare, ourselves to others. Humble people put themselves equal to—not below or above—others. We are no less and no more important than anyone else. When you walk into a meeting, do you take over the room or just take a seat? Do you "read the room" for cues about how and where you might fit?

Humble people are also more self-aware. Employees who demonstrate humility probably have an easier time completing an annual self-appraisal, already knowing some of what they need to improve.

But if we're too hard on ourselves, we won't be able to accept positive feedback. Leah came to realize that her negative view of her performance didn't match reality.

Willing to Learn

In the musical *Hamilton*, Alexander Hamilton's rival, Aaron Burr, asks him, "Why do you assume you're the smartest in the room?" Burr suggests that Hamilton "Talk less. Smile more."[2] At some point in our recovery, we realize we're *not* the smartest person in the room, and we don't need or want to be. Humility includes our willingness to learn and drives our ongoing personal and professional development, which is why it's critical to recovery.

Humility has benefits at work. Leah recognized that she wasn't expected to start the new job knowing everything, and she was able to ask questions and make mistakes. When people are willing to learn from mistakes, performance improves over time. Otherwise, we make the same mistakes over and over. Humble teams are more likely to be successful because strengths and weaknesses are out in the open, so tasks are better allocated.[3]

Practicing Temperance

As a virtue, humility is a component of temperance, along with self-regulation.[4] It takes emotional control not to blurt out our ideas at team meetings, criticize customers in public, or lash out during conflicts. No longer the impulsive people we were, we practice restraint.

Being able to manage our feelings and distorted thinking is one way to demonstrate humility. Asking for help is difficult for many of us before and after recovery. We think we can, or should be able to, solve our own problems. Instead, we put our harsh judgments aside—of ourselves and of others—so we can learn. Leah asked for help when she needed it, which required vulnerability. She was a little embarrassed to ask, but that didn't stop her. She could feel embarrassed without cycling into despair.

Making Space

Being humble also means making space for others, including allowing them to have the opportunities they seek. A tenured faculty member in his late-70s refused to retire, despite teaching very few students and not publishing. Without an open position, the department couldn't bring in new faculty. Contrast that situation with the owner of a hardware store who sold the business to two of his employees and stayed on for the transition. Although it was difficult for him to let go of the business he built, he was glad to pass the opportunity on.

We also make space for others' ideas. When we express gratitude for others' contributions, we demonstrate humility, acknowledging that they have new and better ideas. After some time in the job, Leah offers suggestions on how the intake process could be improved. Although she doesn't know all the history, she hopes the staff is humble enough to listen to her ideas and, if they make sense, implement them.

Sometimes making space is literal. As a small person, I often find myself overlooked. A tall person will stand in front of me, blocking my view, as if I weren't there at all. When hospital chaplains and health care workers speak to patients, they might sit alongside or below eye-level rather than stand over and "talk down to" them. In an office, a humble manager avoids standing over someone's desk or sitting at the head of a table, which could be perceived as arrogant.

Arrogance: Too Little Humility

Some of us with addiction issues used arrogance to mask our character weaknesses. People who feel insecure, as though they can't measure up, might have the loudest voice—or false pride. But people who are humble also can have high self-esteem. Think of it this way: With a realistic view of yourself, you don't need to pump yourself up. You know your limitations, and you're not ashamed or afraid of them. You have nothing to hide.

Avoiding arrogance doesn't mean we shouldn't be proud of our achievements. Although pride is considered a deadly sin when it sets us apart or demeans others, feeling proud of where and how we work is part of emotional success.[5] Chris developed an Excel model that improved how marketing managers access client data. Because she spoke confidently, the team invested time to learn the tool and use it in their work. When we're competent at our jobs, we feel good about ourselves and can contribute to larger organizational goals.

Excessive pride leads us to think we're always right or that our way is the only way. People who lack "intellectual humility" can't admit they're wrong.[6] They aren't curious. No matter how much evidence they see, they never change their minds.

Elizabeth Holmes, founder and former CEO of Theranos, a blood-testing company, was convicted of fraud partly because of her inability to admit failure. She refused to listen to regulators and to her own staff who identified problems with the technology. In her defense, some argued that Holmes had the "swagger and bluster" we expect of an entrepreneur and that men are judged differently. That may be true, but prosecutors labeled her lying to investors and customers "egregious."[7]

Similarly, arrogance gets us in trouble when we can't take constructive criticism. We're too easily wounded. A simple suggestion to save time meets a barrage of "I've been doing this job for xx years," or "I'm certified in xx and know what I'm doing."

Consider your typical reaction to feedback. Do you take the feedback as a personal attack ("He hates me" or "He's just jealous of me")? Do you debate the details ("That's not what I said")? Do you ignore feedback that could be useful? Or do you just shut down ("If she's not happy with the project, I just won't do any more work on it" or "I'm gonna quit").[8] All these responses communicate an unwillingness to learn.

Worthlessness: Too Much Humility

Although meekness in some religions is a positive trait, meaning gentleness, patience, and nonretaliation, when meekness edges toward worthlessness, we see a distortion of humility. Particularly in American cultures, we respect people who are self-assured and confident. Obsessing about our weaknesses tells people we're not competent, can't be trusted with important work, and aren't ready to be promoted. We communicate that we are worthless to the organization.

People may downplay their abilities for manipulative reasons. Pretending they can't do something may be a way to slough off work on others. Or they might degrade themselves to get validation or attention. Instead, we don't seek compliments, but we do accept them graciously.

Self-deprecating jokes also can diminish others' view of us. Although funny in some contexts, there's a big difference between saying, "I can't do math" and "I don't know how to calculate the travel distance." The more specific admission communicates that you're willing to learn and opens space for someone else to teach you, which gives *them* a sense of pride in *their* work.

Too much humility could mean humiliation. When we're publicly ridiculed or discriminated against, others are taking advantage of our vulnerabilities. These situations are not the time for the "Let Them" strategy described in the chapter on willingness.

For 20 minutes, a manager berated an employee during a staff meeting. Out of fear or shock or both, no one spoke up. The spectators had their own inner conflict. Perhaps they felt vicariously worthless and shamed, as if they were the person targeted. Or maybe they worried they would be next. Or maybe they felt self-conscious, wondering about their ability to gracefully diffuse the situation. Next, we look at other complex situations demanding humility.

The Narrow Ridge of Humility

Humility seems paradoxical because we admit failures and mistakes but are strong and confident. We find a balance of humility by understanding the context, by distinguishing between individual and team accomplishments, and by knowing our worth. Initiating a conversation about differences is one way to practice humility with a coworker.

Context

The narrow ridge between arrogance and worthlessness is tough to balance, and context always matters. At recovery meetings, we learn to share in a balanced way—not just the mess, but the message. At work, we know to respect and defer to our boss. We voice opinions, but we're politically savvy; we adjust how we communicate depending on industry, roles, personalities, organizational culture, and so on.

The setting matters too. Camille had a great idea that a coworker took credit for during a staff meeting. She let it go because she wasn't that invested in the idea and wanted to preserve the relationship. Another acceptable approach is for her to talk to her colleague privately after the meeting. But she wouldn't stand up during the meeting to claim credit. That seems arrogant, and people would more likely remember her behavior—her outsized reaction—than the initial offense.

Individual and Team Success

We practice humility when we balance individual and team success. During the selection process, job applicants often say "we." Although you might use "we" to sound humble, an employer will want to know what you, specifically, did as part of a team. A skilled interviewer will probe: "What was *your* role?" Your answer explains the experience you can bring to the organization.

One of my former students described a business on her resume. When I asked what her role was, she said tentatively, "founder-ish." It took a few follow-up questions to understand that she started the business, and I had to convince her to write "founder" as her job title. Another student wrote "CEO and president" as his job title for a one-person start-up. Both are extreme examples. Compare these resume descriptions:

- Singlehandedly automated a slow, outdated expense process that caused redundant work. (Arrogant)
- Developed a new expense process by working with accounting staff and consultants; saved 15 hours of the team's time each month. (Humble)
- Met with accounting staff and consultants to reduce time spent completing expense reports; spent six months developing a new process that most staff used. (Worthless)

The humble example is specific and focuses on quantifiable, objective outcomes. The writer also chooses words to emphasize collaboration: "by working with" and "team."

Spending time observing norms will help you figure out the best approach for online platforms. Posting on LinkedIn about an award you won is perfectly fine, but people expect you to express gratitude for the honor and for people who collaborated with or supported you. Complimenting others doesn't take anything away from ourselves. We can feel good about our work *and* help others shine.

Knowing Our Worth

Negotiating a job offer can be a rocky path for humility. In recovery, we know we're worth *something*, but it's hard to know how much when salary or benefits are flexible. To be paid fairly, you don't want to undersell yourself, but you don't want to price yourself out of a job either.

Knowing what a job pays provides external data about what's fair. Glassdoor, PayScale, and Salary.com list typical pay ranges, which salary transparency laws in some parts of the United States require employers to provide. Some of these laws also prevent an employer from asking about your salary history so you can be paid fairly for the job you're applying for, instead of basing pay on past, lower salaries, particularly if you're switching careers or were out of the workforce for a while.

Humility means accurately assessing your assets, and negotiating for a job is the time to highlight your strengths. You can do this by giving specific examples of why you deserve higher pay. Focus on what the employer would value, for example, experience at a competitor or working with hostile customers. Convince the employer that you're highly motivated and will work hard, but don't just say it; give examples of how you have exceeded expectations in other jobs or service work.[9] Try to avoid arrogance ("You won't find anyone better than me") and worthlessness ("I hope I can learn on the job").

Openness to Other Opinions

Having a difference of opinion with someone challenges our ability to make space for others, and initiating a conversation is good practice for developing humility. Being open means we could change our minds—that the other person could persuade us to think differently.[10] However, this doesn't mean we have to accept others' ideas. During a conversation, we can hold fast to our own thoughts and beliefs—maybe even deepen them—while listening to others.

Zander, a fundraiser, struggled with the organization's philosophy of giving. From Zander's experience, he believed that relationships with donors were cultivated over time, but the organization he recently joined had a much more aggressive approach. He was expected to ask for large donations, even when meeting people for the first time. His manager was clearly angry with him but didn't explain the rationale, so Zander decided to ask.

To understand his manager's perspective, Zander used several interpersonal skills. He approached the situation with curiosity, wondering, "What do they know about the organization and about donors that I need to know?" He used a technique called "zoom in, zoom out," which reminded him to see both the big picture and the details.[11] He saw both the organizational context—its goals, demographics, and so on—and what he would need to do differently to be successful.

During the conversation, Zander tried to get perspective. He carefully observed how his manager was reacting to him and saw that he was getting annoyed. Zander then checked in with himself: How do I feel? What is my body signaling to me? How might my emotional or physical reactions be affecting this interaction? Zander stayed calm, despite his manager's frustration. He considered addressing the frustration but decided to cut the conversation short.

In the end, Zander understood the giving philosophy but didn't feel like a fit for the job. His strength was in long-term relationship building, and it felt wrong for him to approach donors too soon. With humility, he found a different job and then resigned.

Closing Thoughts

Bill W. wrote, "Indeed, the attainment of humility is the foundation principle of each of AA's Twelve Steps. For without some degree of humility, no alcoholic can stay sober at all."[12]

Being humble means that we continue to learn. We're never "one and done" with the steps, and we don't stop going to meetings. The same is true for work: We are always learning something new, both technical skills and in our interactions with others.

Over time, we feel more grounded and more attuned to those around us. Less and less self-centered, we focus on others, including their pain and suffering, which we explore next.

Reflection Questions

1. Describe someone you have worked with who demonstrated humility. What did they say or do?
2. When have you demonstrated humility? Think about a few times in your work life when others may have said that you modeled this principle well.
3. Think about a time when you were arrogant at work. What would you do differently today?
4. How have you represented yourself for a job or promotion in the past that may have come across as either arrogant or worthless? Have you been able to find a better balance since?
5. What's a situation that you could approach with more openness and curiosity? What steps can you take to learn more about a point of view that conflicts with yours?

CHAPTER 8

Compassion

Chapter Overview

When we focus our attention on others instead of ourselves, we can offer compassion to people who are suffering or hurt. Instead of being apathetic, we take notice and take action to demonstrate kindness, common humanity, and mindfulness. To be helpful and to protect ourselves, we don't feel everything the other is feeling; we don't need to be in agony ourselves. At work, we face limits on how much compassion we're able to give and how much is appropriate. But we offer support before harsh judgment.

Rosa's Dilemma

Everyone at work feels hurt at some point and needs compassion. Here's Rosa's story:

> When I was teaching at an elementary school, I had a student who was a real handful. She was always causing trouble—interrupting me and disrupting the class. It was tough for me to do my job.
>
> One day, I lost it. I was told never to cry in front of students, but I couldn't help it. I went into the hallway to try to get my composure.
>
> Another teacher came by and took me around a corner where we were out of view. She just stood with me for a while. I don't even remember what she said, but I felt seen and understood. It was nice to be recognized, and I felt comforted.

Rosa describes the value of compassion. During recovery, we learn to offer and receive support, and now we practice comforting others at work.

Compassion at Work

By the time we take Step Eight, we have an accurate assessment of ourselves and are ready to work on our relationships. We focus our attention on others and demonstrate compassion—not just for those we have harmed but for anyone who is hurting. We determine who needs support and get skilled at providing what they need, which may be only our presence. We extend this care to ourselves when we practice self-compassion.

Alleviating Suffering

When we evolve from our self-centered ways, we start to notice others. In recovery, we welcome the newcomer, listen to their story, and share our own. Compassion is part of our humanity—what unites us as humans and how we show kindness and consideration for others. In a sense, Twelve Step programs are built around compassion from people who understand one another's situation.

Compassion is about alleviating others' suffering, or their hurt, pain, or misfortune. We take time to respond to others by noticing their distress, understanding what they're experiencing, feeling concern, and taking action.[1] Compassion includes the following components:

- Mindfulness (not disengagement): for example, carefully listening to people talk about their troubles
- Common Humanity (not separation): for example, recognizing that everyone feels pain, despite our differences.
- Kindness (not indifference): for example, comforting people when they're sad[2]

Compassion is different from other ways we show concern. Sympathy and pity typically mean feeling sorry for people, which can be demeaning. When we offer compassion, we're also humble—at the same level as others, not looking down on them. Empathy is feeling others' pain, which can be useful but has limitations. Later, we explore these differences as part of the narrow ridge.

Appraisals

When we take Step Eight, we list people we have harmed. Similarly, we discern who needs compassion at work. We may see an obvious sign, for example, a coworker crying, as Rosa's colleague saw, or something more subtle and ambiguous, for example, a coworker who is distracted. For either, we could ignore the situation or take action. Factoring into our appraisal is our judgment: Is the person worthy of compassion?[3]

Everyone knew that Antonio's wife had cancer and that they had three young children. At first, people gave him a lot of slack at work and filled in when they could. But after four years, people became frustrated. When a new employee mentioned Antonio's situation to a coworker, the coworker rolled his eyes and said, "Yeah, his wife has been dying for four years." Depending on the person and context, we decide whether someone deserves our help.

We also might appraise how a person's tragedy affects us. Does it make us a little happy that someone is suffering? When someone is hurting, we do our best to put aside our own feelings to offer support.

Approaches

For some, giving and receiving compassion can feel awkward. The best approach is to start with a conversation, even if it's uncomfortable. You can start with something like, "I've been thinking about you," or "I notice you seem down. Do you want to talk about it?" Sometimes people appreciate just having their pain acknowledged and taking the space to talk. Or, like Rosa, they may appreciate having someone simply stand next to them.

People find validation of their feelings to be more comforting and helpful than other types of responses. Try to listen to what's not said —what the person feels. You can say something like, "I get why you responded like that," "I can imagine that was difficult," or "That would bother me too."[4]

As sponsors or fellow travelers, we support others in recovery by sharing our "own experience, strength, and hope,"[5] as we say in meetings. But that may not be appropriate or appreciated in work situations. Be careful about "taking over" a conversation by talking about yourself instead of giving your full attention to the person hurting.

Depending on the situation, you might try other strategies. People may find comfort in hearing that a situation is temporary and will likely improve, unless it sounds dismissive.[6] Sayings like "This too shall pass" may be best reserved for the rooms of recovery.

Everyone's different. Cultural, relational, industry, situational, and other factors determine the best approach for the person at the time. Some people want company, while others want to be left alone. When Marguerite's husband died suddenly, she felt isolated at work. She wanted to talk about it, but people avoided her and said nothing, which made her feel worse. It's best to ask rather than make assumptions.

Self-Compassion

You may find it easier to show compassion toward others than toward yourself. Self-compassion means caring for yourself, particularly when you experience failure and when you're hurting. This self-care may improve emotional resilience, meaning we're better able to manage through suffering in the future.[7] When we practice self-compassion, we tend to push through instead of being undone by our setbacks.

Researchers define three aspects of self-compassion similar to those of compassion toward others:

- Mindfulness: holding one's experience in balanced perspective rather than exaggerating the dramatic storyline of suffering
- Common Humanity: recognizing that imperfection is a shared aspect of the human experience rather than feeling isolated by one's failures

- Self-Kindness: the ability to treat oneself with care rather than harsh self-judgment[8]

To practice self-compassion, try distancing yourself from negative thoughts and feelings about yourself. What would a friend say about you? How would they offer you comfort that demonstrates mindfulness, common humanity, and self-kindness?[9] When Rosa reflects on her situation at school, she speaks with self-compassion. She doesn't disparage herself for crying but sees it as a natural, human response.

In times of failure, try not to obsess about what you did wrong. Instead, think of what happened as a learning opportunity. Repeatedly asking yourself "*Why* did I do that?" (or "*Why* am I such an idiot?") keeps you stuck in analyzing what went wrong in the past.[10] To focus on learning for the future, ask "*What* can I do differently?" or "*How* can I do better next time?" This strategy works for performance feedback too. Instead of "*Why* didn't I get the foreman position?" which puts the supervisor on the defense, ask, "*What* can I do to prepare myself for the job in the future?" or "*How* can I make myself a better candidate next time there's an opening?"

Psychologists also suggest talking to yourself without saying "I." Try "you" or a third-person pronoun to distance yourself. Instead of "I did this stupid thing," try, "You were hurt and reacted too quickly" or ask, "What happened in the meeting that caused William to react the way he did?" It sounds funny to use your own name but could give you some perspective without being too hard on yourself.[11]

Apathy: Too Little Compassion

We know that compassion eases suffering, but people may still be reluctant to offer it. In addition to the appraisals mentioned earlier, several other issues get in the way of compassion. Too focused on ourselves and our own problems, we might not notice when someone needs our support. Or we might think that we don't have the skills to offer compassion and would make things worse. Or we might not want to expose our own feelings and vulnerabilities. Or our lives may lack feeling, altogether; we might feel numb. To be apathetic is to be without feeling or emotion.

We also might judge people for their suffering. As people with addiction histories, we can be experts at causing our own problems. The same is true for people we work with every day. Someone who fell because she didn't follow safety guidelines still deserves compassion. A broken leg is a broken leg regardless of the cause and our judgment. In recovery, we meet plenty of people who frustrate and annoy us. But we "place principles before personalities";[12] we suspend our negative thinking about the person and help.

Rosa may need help with classroom management. Maybe she can do something differently to change the student's behavior. But her colleague doesn't lecture her about that while she's crying. First, we offer compassion. Later, we can offer suggestions if appropriate.

Psychology research shows that we can develop positive emotions and self-compassion by practicing loving-kindness meditation.[13] During this practice, we send positive thoughts to ourselves and others. We might say something like, "May you be happy," or "May you be free from suffering." Even for those we dislike, we can say, "May you find peace." Over time, meditation decreases our attachment to things in the present, which makes it easier to focus on a positive future. Compassion becomes easier to access and more automatic.[14]

Some people at work go beyond lacking compassion and actually cause suffering, which is worse than apathy. Insensitive comments, unrealistic work demands, or worse create a hostile environment where teams may need to support each other just to get through the day.

Agony: Too Much Compassion

An extreme of compassion is agony—suffering ourselves to the point of being the opposite of apathetic, or *pathetic*. No good would come of Rosa's colleague crying along with her. If she had, she might have turned attention to herself and neglected Rosa's suffering, or she might have embarrassed both of them. In some cases, managers cry while firing or laying off employees; they come across as self-focused and pandering.

For people who feel more acutely, as some of us with addiction histories do, suffering is like wearing an old blanket. Suffering itself becomes a comfort. We love commiserating with other people because we love to be miserable ourselves. But, as the saying goes, pain is inevitable, suffering is optional.[15] How we respond to our own and others' pain is within our control: We can magnify it or manage through with resilience.

When we offer compassion, we can be engaged yet keep a healthy distance. Compassion is acknowledging others' emotions and being there for them. Contrast that with empathy, which means feeling *with* someone and taking on their emotions ourselves. If we take empathy to an extreme when someone is hurting, it's distressful for us, particularly if we're unable to help. Our feelings may become overwhelmingly negative, and we want to disengage as a result.[16] Instead, we can support others without absorbing their emotions.

We can be helpful to people at work as we have been helpful to people in recovery. This requires a measure of emotional restraint and clear boundaries between ourselves and others. Many of us left a life of agony; we don't need to go back there.

The Narrow Ridge of Compassion

Offering compassion that's helpful is a skill anyone can develop. Yet we all have limits and balance compassion and accountability. Receiving compassion can be difficult, partly because we compartmentalize our lives, which is adaptive—to a point.

Our Capacity

Compassion comes more easily to some of us than others. People from a lower socioeconomic status may have an easier time than people from a higher socioeconomic status. One theory is that people with lower incomes need to develop relationships to get by and to manage threats.[17] Stereotypically, you might think women are more compassionate than men, but men may be just as empathic as women[18] and might express comfort differently.

Like most of the principles in Twelve Step programs, showing compassion toward others is a skill. Through meditation and other practices, we get better at comforting people rather than ignoring their pain or getting overwrought ourselves. When we recognize that simply being there for someone may be all they need, comfort can come easily. As Rosa said about her time with her colleague at school, "It was an intimate moment."

We don't need to fix anything. Our tendency to solve people's problems can get in the way of our offering comfort.[19] Although it may be difficult for us to accept, our role isn't to take away their pain. People may need to live through their pain and find their own solutions. Our advice may not be needed or welcomed.

Compassion takes time and requires patience. We tend to move quickly, particularly if we have work to do, but sometimes, the care is the work. When comforting someone who is hurting, we keep our voice slow and low and allow for silence.

Limitations

We don't have to be experts to offer compassion, but some situations require more than we can give. Chronic health issues and financial difficulties cannot be solved by a caring coworker alone. HR departments and employee assistance programs are best equipped to handle these special cases.

Leaders have to balance compassion and accountability. Compassion tends to help people persevere; without feeling shame and despair, they try harder and may perform better.[20] But everyone has limits. All the comfort in the world won't help someone learn a job that's too difficult for them. Leaders shouldn't ignore suffering, yet indulging it can stifle motivation and mask insurmountable performance problems.

Compartmentalizing

In active addiction, we were experts at keeping our personal and professional lives separate. Because of shame, we would buckle up as much as possible to hide our hangover and our using.

Some compartmentalization is useful. We have to get on with our lives despite our troubles. In addition, going to work can be a salve for grief or problems at home. But we find a balance, so we don't shut ourselves off completely. In recovery, we strive to be more integrated people. We can allow our personal lives to seep, a little bit, into the workplace so we can receive compassion.

The skill is to be honest and authentic, while not overwhelming coworkers or making too many excuses for missed work or failures. Obvious issues, for example, wearing a cast or being visibly pregnant, warrant acknowledgment and allow people to offer compassion or congratulate us. This makes us human. But constantly complaining about a personal issue detracts from work and wears coworkers down, particularly when they can do nothing to help.

When debating whether to share personal information at work, you may question your motives. What do you want? Asking for comfort and space is fine. Asking for some flexibility or for someone to fill in for you is fine. But seeking pity or for others to take over work for an extended period of time might be an imposition and show a lack of humility, as if you're above others because of your circumstance.

On the other hand, withholding personal information might also show a lack of humility. Are you trying to be perfect at work, enveloping yourself with "professionalism" and giving the impression that you're better than your coworkers because, unlike them, you can manage your problems on your own? Do you share only positive personal information but nothing negative? You may be separating yourself and denying yourself needed comfort and help. These are difficult judgment calls and are best assessed by advice from others.

Some of us with addiction histories might think that we don't deserve others' support, particularly if we judge ourselves harshly. We're used to muscling through on our own. As recovering isolators, we don't let people see our pain, no less acknowledge or do something about it. Or we mistrust people's intentions. After years of being told to control our addiction, we're skeptical about how someone can be genuinely caring.

Rosa serves as an example. She was able to relax into her colleague's concern. She was able to receive the comfort she needed.

Closing Thoughts

Steps Eight and Nine are often the most difficult for people in Twelve Step programs. We turn our attention to people we harmed and try to make things right. Like offering compassion, we don't always know whether our efforts are helpful, but we do our best. Caring for others takes patience and practice.

Compassion can feel strange at work. We might easily comfort family, friends, and others in recovery, but caring for coworkers requires different skills. We put aside our judgment—and our current tasks— and make ourselves available. Still, knowing when it's enough and when to focus back on work can be challenging. Next, we explore accountability in more detail.

Reflection Questions

1. Think about a time when you comforted someone at work. How did you notice they were in distress? What did you say or do?

2. When were you comforted at work? What was helpful? What wasn't helpful?

3. What makes you hesitant to offer compassion? Think of a time when you may have been helpful but thought twice about it. What held you back?

4. At some point in your life, have you felt apathetic to your own and others' feelings at work? How did you get reengaged or find connection?

5. How can you be more attentive to people at work? What could help you notice others and what they're experiencing?

6. How would you explain the difference between empathy and compassion?

7. How could you demonstrate more self-compassion? What could you do to comfort yourself?

CHAPTER 9

Accountability

Chapter Overview

When we take Step Nine, we take responsibility for our failings and try to repair our relationships. At work, organizational policies, procedures, and expectations guide us, but we find motivation within ourselves to be accountable, which means doing our best work and apologizing for mistakes. We aren't irresponsible; we don't leave messes for others. But we don't clean up others' messes either. We avoid using accountability to manipulate others; we forgive, adjust to what different people need, and both care for and challenge coworkers.

Yon's Dilemma

In possibly the most dreaded of all steps, we make amends to people when we take Step Nine. At work, we take responsibility when things go wrong. Here's Yon's story:

> I was working in a research lab analyzing 16 terabytes of data. That's a lot, and it was all on an external drive. After 10 months on the project, I kept getting error messages and could no longer access the data. At the time, I didn't know whether I completely lost the data, all my work, or both. I wanted to restart the drive, but it was risky because I could lose everything permanently.
>
> Instead, I told my manager about it. I immediately apologized—not that it was my fault (I was pretty sure I didn't do anything wrong), but I was sorry about the situation. I guess I also apologized because I wanted to show that I understood the impact and would take responsibility for finding a solution.

I called the external drive company, and they couldn't retrieve the data. Unfortunately, it wasn't backed up anywhere. Early in the project, we talked about the risk, and my manager said it wasn't worth the expense. So that was his decision.

Fortunately, there was a happy ending. I reluctantly (and with my manager's permission) restarted the drive, and all was well. But what a scare I had, and I was glad I didn't make the situation worse by trying to hide what happened.

A common work expression is, "If you're not part of the solution, you're part of the problem." We take responsibility regardless of whether we're at fault.

Accountability at Work

Being accountable means taking responsibility. We take direction from others at work yet take initiative to solve problems when they happen. Just as we do in a Twelve Step program, we apologize when we're at fault and make living amends when apologies aren't possible.

Responsibility

When we make amends to people, we're taking responsibility for harm we have done and commit to doing better. To amend is to "repair" or "set right."[1]

In work environments, we think of accountability as taking ownership and committing to action, even if we didn't cause the problem. Accountability is both a response and an accounting—our choice to *respond* to a need and an *account* or explanation of our role. Technology problems happen; even though Yon wasn't responsible for the error messages, he took responsibility for the solution.

Earlier we discussed transparency as part of integrity—disclosing relevant information clearly and accurately. When Yon is accountable, he is also communicating openly with his manager. Allison, a social media manager, said accountability was one of the biggest lessons she learned when working her first job. If she made a mistake, she tried to "get ahead of it." She knew it was worse if she waited until her boss found out and then came to her with questions. At that point, she was on the defensive about what happened—and she had to explain why she didn't come forward earlier.

People who are accountable at work are respected. In active addiction, many of us were irresponsible. By missing work or deadlines, we showed people we couldn't be counted on. Accountable people are reliable and proactive—the ones who solve problems and get things done. They manage other people in addition to their own work.

External Pressure

So far, we talked about what we can do as employees to hold ourselves accountable. But employees are also held accountable by managers and systems. A rolling conveyor belt, computer monitoring, sales goals, mystery shoppers, client caseloads, and patient rounds are all performance metrics, and they are all stressors. Managers of people and projects have their own stress. They're expected to keep their team staffed, developed, and satisfied; manage resources well; ensure compliance; and meet strategic goals.

We may see this stress as positive or negative. Some measures feel motivational. Performance targets or "stretch goals" inspire us to learn and work harder because they challenge us and can contribute to our career success. These motivations result in greater loyalty to an organization, higher job satisfaction, and better performance.[2]

But strict organizational policies and time measures can cause people to feel negatively stressed. They worry about being punished[3] and lose common sense.[4] Amazon finally changed how it measures "time off task," which reportedly caused some warehouse employees to avoid taking bathroom breaks.[5] We have little control over this type of pressure.

How we attribute a failure can cause us more stress. Paradoxically, if we blame external forces, we create more stress for ourselves because we can't do anything about it.[6] But when we can identify our own responsibility and choose how to change course, we actually feel less stress. Taking responsibility helped Allison feel better because she could fix whatever part of a problem she caused and bring possible solutions to her boss, which he wanted to hear so *he* could take action if needed. Our task is to discern our contribution to a failure, and then we need to apologize.

Apologies

Step Nine tells us to "make direct amends to such people wherever possible, except when to do so would injure them or others." In common language, this is apologizing, which is expected when people make mistakes at work. We may feel the same at work as we did during those awkward Step Nine conversations—wobbly and exposed. But the purpose is the same: to admit where we went wrong and begin to repair the damage, including relationships. The admission is the first step in finding a solution.

In recovery, we don't strive for specific outcomes from our apologies; our goal isn't, for example, to save a marriage or get someone to apologize to us in return. But, at work, of course we want our apology to have some effect. We want the receiver to trust us—to know that they can depend on us to solve the problem and to not cause the same problem in the future. We want better relations and to be forgiven, so others are no longer angry, resentful, or wanting revenge.

Social psychologists have identified eight components of sincere apologies. When an apology has many of the following elements that address the receiver's needs, the receiver is more likely to forgive: showing remorse (e.g., saying, "I'm sorry" or "I apologize" instead of "I regret"), accepting responsibility (e.g., saying, "It's my fault," or "I failed to"), saying what you did wrong, explaining what happened, acknowledging the impact, offering to fix it, saying what you'll do differently, and requesting forgiveness. Sincere apologies avoid the following tactics, which are more self- than other-focused: making excuses, justifying our actions, blaming the victim, and minimizing the impact.[7]

We should avoid explanations if they are defensive. For example, Allison might say, "I forgot to call the client because I didn't have a reminder set up," but not, "I didn't call the client because it's so hard to set up reminders in the system." She could say, "I have trouble setting up reminders and could use help so this doesn't happen in the future." Part of the value of an apology is the opportunity to ask for help.

Our apologies come across as more sincere when they are, in fact, sincere. If you were short with a customer and genuinely feel sorry, you'll make a better apology, not because you're following the apology guidelines as a checklist but because you'll naturally include more of the positive and fewer of the negative elements. Empathy makes us more likely to apologize well—and receive forgiveness,[8] which we'll discuss later.

Living Amends

When a good friend of mine died of bulimia, it felt impossible for me to make amends to her. For years, because of my own eating disorders, I was oblivious to her struggle, which she hid well, but not that well. To make amends, I wrote her a letter and, once a year, I sit by her grave to apologize. I also spoke openly about my history and started a local peer support group. This is the best I felt I could do.

Living amends is about our commitment to change. In active addiction 15 years ago, Maryam took a stapler from her employer. She returned it with a note but later felt silly about it and thought she might have done something more meaningful instead, for example, donating to a nonprofit school. She also might be extra-diligent in how she currently accounts for her organization's finances, living in a new way.

Living amends may be as simple as approaching work and relationships differently. We can't change being difficult in the past, but we can be more conscientious teammates now. Intentional living amends are far better than irresponsibility, or avoiding issues entirely.

Irresponsibility: Too Little Accountability

Some work cultures make it difficult for employees to be accountable. When managers are overly punitive and shaming, employees tend to do the bare minimum. Similarly, risk-averse organizations cause employees to live in fear of making mistakes and hide them when they inevitably happen. A blaming culture in health care fails to improve patient safety. A risk-adverse tech culture squelches innovation. Accountable employees accept the consequences of their decisions, but if they are punished for negative results, they might not make any decisions at all.

In organizations that accept failures as part of learning, taking responsibility for failure is easier. Yet we still may deny failures because we succumb to our fears and character weaknesses. Earlier steps guided us through letting go of behaviors and thought patterns that had protected but no longer serve us. By the time we take Step Nine, we no longer see ourselves as victims. We don't need excuses for failures, for example, unclear communication or unreasonable expectations, which will always be the case at work. Instead, we control what we can—our own actions and reactions.

Although painful, negative emotions can inspire healthy reactions to failure. Feeling our feelings offers better outcomes than cognitive approaches. *Thinking* about what went wrong and why it happened can lead to rationalizing a failure—finding reasons that protect us, as Allison would have done if she had blamed the system for her client mistake. But allowing ourselves to be sad and reflecting on our feelings about a failure may lead to more learning; we'll be less likely to make the same mistake in the future.[9]

In addition to owning our failures, being accountable means doing our best work. In a work environment with little accountability, we can still hold ourselves to high standards. This is a service to an organization with abundant resources or weak leadership. We can lead, serving as a role model for others. A political appointee, Anya says she had "no management" and had to keep herself active and motivated. She focused on the communities she served and set a higher bar for others in similar positions.

Quiet quitting—doing less and less over time or doing the least possible work to get by—is irresponsible. If we regularly do less than what is expected of us and what we're capable of, people may expect less of us over time, which creates a cycle of underperformance and low expectations. Earlier, you read about Lydia, Alex's assistant, who only ordered supplies and minimized interruptions. Lydia did very little, which was how Alex trained her, and that was Alex's failing. But Lydia also shirked responsibility. She accepted and performed to low expectations. Maybe she feared that she couldn't do more or wasn't motivated to try. Whatever the reason, her job became so narrow that she wasn't accountable for much.

Worse than quiet quitting is not giving a shit. This popular advice seems to encourage us to lean into our resentments and bask in our anger. Instead of disengagement, we use our recovery skills to accept what we can't change, find courage to address what we can, and be accountable for ourselves and how we show up to work.

Manipulation: Too Much Accountability

When we take too much accountability, we don't hold others responsible. What can seem like kindness, for example, covering for someone whose performance isn't measuring up, relieves them of consequences that may be appropriate, even helpful in the long run. Although Alex may have tried to protect Lydia by expecting less of her or overfunctioning for her, she ultimately hurt her—prevented her from getting training or coaching she needed, or from getting into a role that was more suitable. In the end, Alex manipulated, or controlled, the outcome for her.

As people in recovery, we know how others covered for us, which may have felt helpful at the time but only delayed our getting the help we needed. In these cases, others manipulated consequences for us, and we let them. We could say that people who act irresponsibly leave a mess for others, while people who take too much responsibility clean up everyone else's mess.

Overapologizing can have a similar effect. In her book *A Woman's Way through the Twelve Steps*, Stephanie Covington warns us not to let people off the hook too easily. What are we apologizing for when someone harms us? Instead, we could say that we were wronged and maybe that we reacted in a way that wasn't helpful. Or, we may see that we don't owe an apology at all.[10]

I have tripped over myself apologizing, only to realize later that I did nothing wrong. In one case, I was accused of publicly attacking someone. I immediately, tearfully apologized. But later, it didn't sit right with me. I checked with others who overheard, and no one else interpreted my comment that way. I felt manipulated—that my coworker was dealing with her own feelings about herself and projected them onto me. My hasty apology prevented her from exploring her own reactions to what I said. Covington warns, ". . . when we don't hold others accountable, we're often too ready to believe that we caused or provoked someone else's behavior—or even deserved the abuse we received."[11]

When we take Step Nine, we're warned not to make amends if we would do more harm than good. What are our motives if we force someone to relive a situation they would rather forget? If we want to be showered with gratitude and complimented on our recovery, then our motives are skewed. We may be overdoing the *appearance* of accountability, with the focus on ourselves.

The Narrow Ridge of Accountability

When we forgive ourselves and others, we lift burdens of negative emotions. We use different approaches to take and assign responsibility based on the context and person. The goal is to create a culture of accountability that facilitates learning and growth.

Forgiveness

Forgiveness is one way to navigate the narrow ridge between irresponsibility and manipulation. When we forgive, we let go of our anger and resentments. To resent means to "feel pain, regret" and to "feel again."[12] When we hold onto resentments, we cause ourselves to feel bad feelings over and over. As the saying goes, "Resentment is like taking poison and waiting for the other person to die."

Forgiveness can be both a trait and a state.[13] As a trait, forgiveness means living a life mostly free of anger and resentment—not seeking revenge or holding onto grudges. We hold people responsible, but we don't blame and shame them as a result of our own negative feelings toward them. As a state, forgiveness is situational. We forgive for something specific.

We might resist forgiving others, believing it releases the other from responsibility. But that's not the case; it releases *us* from obsession and from psychological and, for some, physical pain.[14] Once we forgive, we become responsible for our own feelings and actions. We might see that we denied our own contribution to a problem, or we might see that we made excuses for the other and took too much on ourselves. Forgiveness allows for greater understanding and puts a situation in perspective.

We also forgive ourselves. Recognizing our own transgressions frees us up, so we're no longer obsessing about what we did wrong and can focus on how to change. Also, if we want to be forgiven, we need to forgive ourselves first.

I finally forgave myself for not noticing my friend's eating disorder. About a year after her death, I had a dream that I expressed my concern to her, and she shrugged it off. After that and hearing that others had tried to talk with her, I realized I may not have had an impact, anyway. I had been feeling extremes of the narrow ridge—both irresponsible because I hadn't taken action and overly responsible, as though I could have magically lifted her addiction, manipulating the outcome that was probably inevitable. I released myself and, in a sense, released her; I was no longer trying to control her fate.

Accountability Continuum

At work, we balance external and internal measures of accountability. Although organizational policies can be too restricting, a work culture that allows employees to set their own schedules and performance goals isn't always practical. Instead, we can think of accountability on a continuum, which is adjusted for different employees at different times. A new employee needs more support and direction and will benefit from checklists and regular coaching. After learning the job, they can work more independently. Someone with experience needs less direction than someone new to the industry.

Imagine Samuel, who is back in the workforce after six months in rehab. He may need more direction and more frequent check-ins to stay on task until his confidence builds. Punitive micromanaging won't inspire Samuel; a good leader will move him toward greater independence so he can hold himself accountable. Samuel will learn when he needs help, and he'll ask for it, hoping that his manager patiently and collaboratively solves problems with him.

A manager I know said, "I learned that I don't need my staff to be the best employees for me. I need to be the best leader for them." She meant that she adjusts how she leads based on each employee's needs at the time. Good employees also adjust to their manager and learn how often the manager wants updates and whether they prefer email or other methods of communication. This is part of managing up: In addition to bringing solutions to problems, employees are proactive, taking initiative to build a productive relationship with their manager.

Radical Candor

In her book *Radical Candor*, Kim Scott promotes a working culture where people care personally and challenge each other directly.[15] She describes a narrow ridge that includes both. With underlying trust and good personal relationships, team members have an easier time giving and receiving tough feedback. People are held responsible and hold themselves accountable because they know that their coworkers want the best for them and will support but not coddle them. In recovery, we might be fortunate enough to feel both cared for and challenged by a sponsor.

Kim Scott gives the simple example of seeing someone at work with their fly down. If you care too much and can't challenge the person, you say nothing because you feel embarrassed for them, or you're too worried about your own feelings and how the person may react to you. Maybe you make it worse by whispering about them to a coworker. If you're too challenging, you might be a jerk and embarrass the person, yelling across the room that their fly is down.

Scott encourages radical candor: You subtly whisper to the person that their fly is down. She encourages difficult conversations even if someone is hurt or emotional during the interaction. After healthy time in recovery, we know how to handle our own and others' feelings. We rise to the challenge instead of avoiding those tough conversations. That's how, over time, we build a culture of accountability at work.

Closing Thoughts

Bill W. writes about a narrow ridge for making amends. He refers to the "AA beam,"[16] the need for good judgment rather than adjusting our amends based on people's potential reactions—either positive or negative. At work, we neither shirk our responsibilities nor come across like a ton of bricks. We accept consequences of our actions regardless of additional consequences we might face in the process of taking responsibility.

When we work the steps, we "clear away the wreckage of the past."[17] We also clear new wreckage that we create as we live our human lives. Our goal is always for better relationships. Next, we explore the last three steps, and our focus turns to sustaining ourselves and the greater community.

Reflection Questions

1. Think about a time when you took responsibility for something that was or wasn't your fault. How did you handle the situation, and how did it turn out?

2. What's an example of a living amends you're making at work?

3. Think about a time when you didn't take responsibility for something that was your fault. What caused you to avoid stepping up? What might you do differently today?

4. How could you hold yourself more accountable in your job, without external measures?

5. In what ways might you be too accountable, for example, by making excuses or covering up for others? How do you see this as potentially manipulative?

6. In what ways could you encourage a culture of greater accountability in your current workplace? Think about your own responsibility and how you might influence others.

SECTION 4

We Sustain Ourselves and the Greater Community

STEP	DEFICIENCY (too little)	PRINCIPLE	EXCESS (too much)
10. Continued to take personal inventory and when we were wrong promptly admitted it.	Laziness	Perseverance	Perfectionism
11. Sought through prayer and meditation to improve our conscious contact with God *as we understood Him*, praying only for knowledge of His will for us and the power to carry that out.	Self-absorption	Spiritual Awareness	Fundamentalism
12. Having had a spiritual awakening as the result of these Steps, we tried to carry this message to _____, and to practice these principles in all our affairs.	Ingratitude	Service	Suffocation

The last three steps invite us to reach further inside and further outside ourselves. We deepen our self-awareness with daily reflection, feel broader connections, and extend service to others. As we progress in our recovery, we become role models within our communities, including our community at work.

We find motivation within ourselves to persevere at work, yet we know when to quit so we don't do more damage than good. We continue to come out of ourselves and form connections to people we work with, which may extend beyond the work itself. To avoid future resentments, we check our expectations and our rigidity and instead find gratitude and service to sustain ourselves and contribute to a positive, generative working environment.

CHAPTER 10

Perseverance

Chapter Overview

As the first of the three maintenance steps, Step 10 encourages daily reflection and continuous improvement. We avoid laziness by persevering—working to overcome obstacles to reach long-term goals. With a healthy drive, we pursue excellence but stop short of perfectionism. Instead, we manage our work–life balance, discover when to quit, and develop habits that move us closer to achieving our goals.

Shana's Dilemma

Many of us with addiction histories have overcome obstacles, and we continue to face barriers. Here's Shana's story:

> I always had trouble reading. Growing up, my teachers told me I had dyslexia, although it was never confirmed. I couldn't sit long enough to take the test because of my anxiety. I didn't do well in school and was put into the "special" classes. I used to memorize reading passages so when I was called on in class, I could recite them without the other kids making fun of me.
>
> When I said I wanted to go to college, my guidance counselor said, "Your parents may be wasting their money. You're not that smart." Well, I did go to college and managed to have a successful yoga business. But I wanted to do deeper, more clinical work and accept insurance so I could work with more people.
>
> It took me 20 years to work up the nerve to pursue a master's degree in clinical social work. I got into a great program, and now I'm a student again. It's not easy for me, but I use my

own yoga and breathing practice to manage my anxiety, and I allow myself more time for the assigned readings. I know I'll get through it.

Shana describes perseverance, removing barriers to her long-term goals. Along the way, she learns about herself, as we do when we take Step 10.

Perseverance at Work

In the first of the maintenance steps we use every day, Step 10 asks us to "continue to take personal inventory." Perseverance requires a drive to work through obstacles to long-term goals. With a daily reflection practice, we develop self-awareness to understand what character strengths and weaknesses need attention.

Sticking With It

As people in recovery, we know what it means to stick with a program. We hear from others who "go to any lengths" to stay sober, and we hear from people in the "no-matter-what club," who stay sober regardless of what happens in their lives. They describe perseverance, overcoming obstacles to pursue long-term personal and professional goals.

Other principles relate to perseverance. Earlier, we explored courage, which means pushing past fear, which is one obstacle we might face. Courage typically applies to in-the-moment or short-term situations, whereas perseverance is more focused on long-term goals—over months or years. We also explored the value of hope to build resilience. Hope reveals paths forward and provides motivation for us to address new and changing obstacles. We may also think of perseverance as faith in action, an internal force to pursue greater goals.

In addition to these principles, perseverance relates to the philosophy of stoicism, which means "unemotional endurance of pain."[1] Stoics valued acceptance, judgment, self-control, tranquility—many of the lessons we learn in recovery.

When we persevere, our own doubts and others' discouragement do not deter us from reaching our goals. When Terrance opened a store to upcycle furniture, he needed funding. He wrote grant after grant trying to win support but had little success. Early days were tight, and at times, he couldn't make payroll. To get more financial backing, he thought of new ideas to diversify funding sources and increase revenue, such as starting a reentry from prison training program and accepting clothes and books. After a few years, Terrance was able to expand his store into three locations that became a model for others. Like Shana, he stuck with it.

Drive and Grit

Even without the funding obstacles, Terrance needed drive to achieve his vision of an upcycle store. A critical part of strong character in the workplace, drive includes striving for excellence, taking initiative, focusing on results, and demonstrating passion.[2]

Motivation and drive are similar, but drive comes from a deeper place. Although motivation can be intrinsic or extrinsic, drive is always internal—a force that propels us forward and, if we're lucky, gives us an abundant supply of energy. At our best, we are driven by the work itself and get satisfaction from overcoming obstacles.

People who have grit—who are gritty—demonstrate both passion and perseverance as they pursue goals. In other words, they have the internal drive to solve problems as they arise. Gritty employees tend to stay longer on the job, feel more engaged at work, and perform at higher levels than those who aren't gritty.[3]

Of course, employers want employees with these qualities. You can demonstrate drive during a hiring process by speaking with enthusiasm in your voice and by highlighting ways in which you have pursued challenging goals. You also might describe how you rebounded after a failure, showing that you're not easily undone by obstacles.

Daily Reflection

As the director of catering for an event planning business, Emmanuel led a team of 14 people to host a dinner for the prime minister of Italy. It was a high-profile event with six buffets, and they were running late.

As soon as they finished setting up each buffet, people were coming around to fill their plates. Fortunately, Emmanuel was able to keep his composure, and all went well. Still, after the event, he reflected on the experience, as we do when we take Step 10, to always try to do better.

A daily reflection practice helps avoid triggers that may cause relapse. As he reviewed the day, Emmanuel caught himself before slipping back into old thought patterns. In the past, he would have blamed traffic and venue management for not letting them set up earlier. His anger and resentment would have led him to numb out by drinking. Instead, reflection put the event into perspective. Yes, they should have left earlier. Yes, they should have negotiated the set-up time. Also, yes, Emmanual led his team clearly and succinctly. They worked efficiently, and nothing was lost or dropped.

You may use an app or develop your own questions for daily reflection. Some people find it useful to spend time reflecting in the morning and in the evening, but any time works as long as it's a routine practice. Questions may include the following: Was I honest today? Did I feel resentful? Was I fearful? Did I do something for someone else today? Did I pray or meditate today? Did I hurt someone? Step 10 also tells us to "promptly admit" when we're wrong.

Consider including task-related questions in a daily reflection: What did I accomplish today? What new skill did I learn or use today? What do I still need to learn? When was I most focused today? When did I cut corners? What was most challenging for me today? Commitment to this daily practice requires discipline and action to build on strengths and address issues as they arise.

Self-Awareness

When we take Step Four, we acknowledge our fears and character weaknesses. Step 10 is a daily practice that, over time, deepens this self-awareness. The goal is to know ourselves as others know us—to have an accurate view of who we are. Character is how others perceive us as whole human beings. Self-awareness is a measure of how well our image of ourselves matches how others see us.

Having an accurate understanding of ourselves requires both internal and external self-awareness. Internal awareness includes how clearly we know what's important to us, how well we understand our reactions, and how we affect others. External awareness is knowing how others perceive us. If you have high internal awareness but low external awareness, you may be highly introspective but have a lot of blind spots; you don't allow for others' perceptions of you. Or maybe you have high external awareness but low internal awareness: You focus on pleasing others—cultivating their image of you—but lack a sense of who you really are. If you have little internal or external self-awareness, you may still be seeking—trying to discover who you are and what others think of you. Ideally, you have both: As a fully aware person, you know yourself and actively seek feedback from others to bring blind spots into view.[4]

Olivia was managing a project for the first time and had a couple of senior-level people on the team. She talked at length and at random times about her previous experience. It felt cloying and distracting to others. When someone spoke with her about how she was coming across, she was surprised, thinking she was building credibility. Instead, she learned to build credibility by focusing on the work.

Full awareness is the value of 360°—or multirater—feedback. In addition to our self-assessment, we receive external feedback for a complete picture of ourselves, and we accept constructive feedback gracefully. Earlier, we discussed defensive reactions to feedback; other reactions aren't helpful either. You might blame yourself too harshly or accept feedback without evidence, even if you don't agree with it. Self-awareness is an iterative process. You decide whether and how to incorporate new information into your self-image. As you do, you persevere more skillfully by using your strengths and learning how to overcome obstacles so you can tackle new challenges.

Laziness: Too Little Perseverance

We're all lazy at times and should be, which we explore later as a narrow ridge topic. But too much laziness, which many of us knew well in active addiction, prevents us from achieving our goals. A popular recovery saying is, "Alcohol [or any substance] gave me the wings to fly and then took away the sky."

Gregory's manager said he was about to get fired. He explained the reason: Gregory hadn't completed any daily time sheets in the past three weeks. Gregory said, "You want me to complete the timesheets? OK, I'll do them." He went to his office and, within 15 minutes, submitted them all. He still got fired.

Why do people neglect work that's expected of them? We procrastinate because of personal and situational reasons. Personal reasons include negative feelings about a task, compounded by negative feelings about procrastination itself.[5] We might delay work because of anxiety, fear of failure (or success), low self-esteem, low (or high) self-confidence, rebellion, shortsightedness, lack of concentration, bad decision making, poor time management, and lots of other reasons.[6] Gregory may have been rebellious, believing that the timesheets were a waste of his time. In recovery, we might consider these reasons character weaknesses—obstacles to overcome.

Situational reasons for procrastination include subgroup expectations, career plateaus, and heavy workload.[7] If no one else on our team is working hard, we might not either, as we discussed in the chapter on accountability. If we don't see opportunities for promotions and salary increases, we might have no reason to push ourselves. We might have a heavy workload—or we might prioritize work that's easy or right in front of us and neglect work that could bring more satisfaction or have greater impact.

We can find ways to push ourselves when we lack the drive. In their book *Designing Your Life*, Bill Burnett and Dave Evans suggest assessing how engaged and energized you feel during events throughout your day. They encourage identifying when you feel "in flow" and "in the zone"—fully involved in something and losing track of time.[8] During these times, you're probably performing well. Feeling competent, or developing mastery, is related to drive.[9] Having a sense of purpose and setting small, achievable goals also may propel you forward.[10] Initial structure and external accountability might give you the boost you need to find your internal drive.

Perfectionism: Too Much Perseverance

A common downside of too much striving is perfectionism. We impose impossible standards on ourselves, project what we think others expect from us, or absorb social messages about how we should be.[11] We become overly demanding of ourselves out of "fear and insecurity" about how our performance or, worse, how we as human beings, will be judged.[12]

Some aspects of perfectionism are positive. Striving for excellence, having high standards, and setting aspirational goals increase motivation and conscientiousness.

But, on balance, perfectionism is harmful. Perfectionism doesn't lead to better performance as you may think; instead, it results in anxiety and burnout.[13] Shana monitors herself: She's ambitious about getting a master's degree, but she doesn't cause herself anxiety by comparing herself to others or by pushing herself too hard. She resists buying into a culture where people boast about being "*so* busy."

Bill W. warns us to "look for progress, not perfection" when we take Step 10.[14] The danger is judging ourselves too critically and regressing into black-and-white thinking. If we miss one question on our daily inventory, why bother doing it at all? Or, at work, we might feel like quitting if we make one mistake.

Perfectionism inevitably leads to disappointment. When career planning, we might be asked to "imagine your ideal job" or "find your passion." This sets us up for one possible outcome, which might not be realistic—and could be a letdown if it's not what we expected. Bryan landed a job with a large, prestigious company. He had an image of what the working environment would be like, but he had a rude awakening. The organization was messy, with lots of bureaucracy and low morale. Organizations are just as fallible as people. Bryan set himself up for disappointment with an idealized version of the company.

A more realistic career planning process includes multiple options. According to Burnett and Evans, "for most people, passion comes *after* they try something, discover they like it, and develop mastery—not before."[15] Expecting to know your passion, particularly as a young person, may discourage or frustrate you. Instead, Burnett and Evans suggest identifying three-to-five career options and "trying stuff" to learn what you like best.[16]

To resist perfectionism, we practice grace and allow for imperfections. With external guidance, we recalibrate our standards and set achievable goals. We try to see setbacks as learning opportunities—not reasons to self-flagellate or quit. We take breaks, allowing ourselves time to get perspective and recharge.

We also try to avoid ruminating, or obsessing, a common practice of perfectionists.[17] In the word *perseveration*, incessantly repeating words or thoughts, we see the same root of perseverance. Instead, we practice mindfulness and self-compassion and focus on positive aspects of our work.

If you can, delegate some parts of your work. Beatrice, a marketing professional with a music side-hustle, usually controlled every part of their gig. But for once, she let another band member create the promotional flyer. Beatrice liked the results even though the flyer wasn't perfect. Giving up some control was good practice for her.

The Narrow Ridge of Perseverance

As we strive for excellence, we balance our personal lives, including our health, and learn when it's best to cut our losses and quit. Developing new habits can reduce how much we struggle to meet our goals.

Work–Life Balance

The most obvious narrow ridge issue for perseverance is work–life balance, minimizing conflicting demands between our professional and personal lives. Pervasive technology—always being connected or "on"—makes it particularly difficult for us to separate work and personal time. We all need time to relax. Taking vacation time without checking email or enjoying a "lazy Sunday" is not lazy.

Problems with work–life balance may be simply working too much. One week after Melissa gave birth, she was asked to go on partial maternity leave. She took her baby to work and held him during meetings. Years later, she regretted not taking the time she wanted with her newborn.

Of course, not everyone has the luxury of working just 40 hours per week. Emerging from addiction, you might need to work a second or third job to get back on your feet, pay off debt, or simply to make ends meet. Finding time to sleep, exercise, eat well, and take breaks is challenging but essential to "work–health balance," which includes managing our health while working.[18] In recovery, that could include going to meetings or calling our sponsor.

The 20 questions of Workaholics Anonymous help identify issues with overwork. This question gets at the narrow ridge, particularly our ambivalence about work: "Are there times when you are motivated and push through tasks when you don't even want to and other times when you procrastinate and avoid them when you would prefer to get things done?" Other questions ask whether we use work to avoid intimacy or feelings of "grief, anxiety, and shame?"[19] If so, we may be overworking.

Knowing When to Quit

Shame can drive us beyond a healthy point. Fear of failure or embarrassment bully us into pursuing a goal that no longer makes sense.

Sometimes, we're in too deep to get out. The "sunk-cost fallacy" causes us to stick with something just because we don't want to lose what we already invested—even if it will cost more in the end. After all the money or time we put into something, we can't seem to cut our losses. Three weeks into a six-week electrician apprenticeship program, Andrew knew the work wasn't for him, but he finished the training—and was back on the job market soon after. This irrational behavior resulted in his missing out on other opportunities.

Knowing when to quit is a gift of the narrow ridge. We aren't slipping and falling; we choose when it's time to stop. In her book *Quit: The Power of Knowing When to Walk Away*, psychologist and retired professional poker player Annie Duke describes the importance of quitting and the difficulty of timing. If you quit too soon, you might regret it; quit too late, and you might suffer more damage.[20] In addition to the sunk-cost fallacy, she says people resist quitting because they prefer the status quo and fear uncertainly. In other words, we stay the course because it's familiar.

Duke suggests taking emotion out of decisions to quit. She recommends setting criteria for quitting up front and evaluating potential long-term outcomes, including how the decision would affect others.[21] In the chapter on hope, you met Jade, the entrepreneur with the dance studio. Emotions certainly factor into her decision about whether to keep the business going. She loves the space and enjoys meeting the few people who come. She feels hopeful but is rational, not excessively optimistic. She considers ramping up marketing and finding partnerships, but she's not hiring a lawyer to set up a franchise.

Developing Habits

Developing habits can help us persevere without overdoing it. When behaviors are repeated over time, they become less dependent on our setting goals and more influenced by automatic action.[22] New habits are formed by, first, creating a routine of behaviors. The more we repeat those actions, the easier they become to take. A fun habit can be developed quickly, but tougher habits will take longer, depending on the person.[23]

Our addiction may have become a habit—shopping during downtime or stopping at the liquor store on the way home from work—but we replace those habits with healthier ones. Shana's long-term goal is completing her master's degree. Every morning, she practices yoga to reduce her anxiety and put her in the right frame of mind for class or for studying. She doesn't wake up and debate whether to do yoga; it's part of her routine, like brushing her teeth.

Our Step 10 daily inventory can become habit, and so can other reflection practices at work. A team can build a postevent or project-end review to evaluate, as Emmanuel did after the catering event, what went well and what could be improved next time. Many organizations have adopted practices such as the military's After-Action Review to understand what happened during critical incidents and to identify changes needed for the future. When a review process is built into the work, it's easier to do before moving on to the next project.

Perseverance doesn't have to feel like a struggle. With good habits and more perspective, we take gentler steps toward our long-term goals and avoid obsessing about how imperfect we are.

Closing Thoughts

Giving up our addiction took perseverance. We were told to "keep coming back," and we did. We're asked to prioritize our sobriety above all else. We're warned that our addiction is doing push-ups—waiting to overtake us—so we build our own resistance.

Now we apply that same perseverance to our work. We put energy into all that engages us, and we don't self-sabotage by setting impossible standards that cause us to fail or give up too soon. As we work, we continue to improve and expand our reach further toward others. Next, we explore how spiritual awareness can support our efforts.

Reflection Questions

1. What questions on your daily inventory are related to work? If you don't have a list, you can create it now.
2. Do you consider yourself more internally or externally self-aware? How could you improve in both areas?
3. Thinking about the last week or so, at what points did you feel flow—engaged and energized by what you were doing? How could you build more flow into your daily life?
4. In what ways are you a perfectionist? How does this ideal motivate you and yet cause you harm?
5. How do you assess your work–life or work–health balance? How would you like to improve the balance, and what can you do about it?
6. Have you stuck with something too long? In retrospect, what would have helped you decide when to quit? Is there something

now in your work that you're considering quitting? What criteria can you use to avoid an emotionally driven decision? How can you seek guidance?

7. What is a positive work habit that you would like to develop? What behavioral routines can you start with and then repeat over and over?

CHAPTER 11

Spiritual Awareness

Chapter Overview

Step 11 is about spiritual awareness, which means something different to everyone. At work, we develop connections that feel like shared, common experiences that transcend the individual. We stand together and face larger forces together. As we improve our self-awareness among others and beyond ourselves, we become less self-absorbed and less fundamentalist, instead gaining perspective that helps us build deeper relationships.

Elizabeth's Dilemma

Sometimes, adversity illustrates our connection to each other. Here's Elizabeth's story:

> I was a vice president at a Fortune 500 company in a large building in New York City. It was almost the end of day when we lost power.
>
> People started gathering in the hallway, which had a little light from generators. I remember some "dark humor" about the end of the world and some nervous laughter, but it was pretty scary not knowing what was going on.
>
> The phone lines weren't working well, but we finally got communication that power was out throughout the city. No trains were running, so people couldn't get home if they left the building. People decided it was safest to stay.
>
> We were hungry. I had an idea that we should get food from the little store in the building. Obviously, the elevators weren't working, so a group of us trudged down eight flights and raided

the store! We felt like bandits, and I figured I would take the blame if I had to. We brought back all the candy and drinks we could carry and went back for more later.

A bunch of us stayed overnight until power got restored that evening and into the next morning. Later we learned there were outages throughout the U.S. Northeast, parts of the Midwest, and into Canada. Our workgroup felt connected forever—and connected to the other 55 million people affected.

Connection is one way to transcend our own circumstance and experience spiritual awareness, and we explore other ways to get greater perspective, particularly during difficult situations.

Spiritual Awareness at Work

Spiritual awareness means many different things to different people. However we experience spirituality, we use tools, such as prayer and meditation, which are recommended for Step 11, to transcend our current situation and thinking beyond ourselves.

Spirituality

Spirituality is personal, grounding us within the universe; it's however we find meaning, peace, purpose, or more. We experience connection with something bigger and other than ourselves. In Step 11, we are less concerned about *what* we connect to and more concerned with how we experience connection. Spirituality can be experienced by praying, walking in nature, going to a recovery meeting, practicing meditation, or dancing. At work, people may experience spirituality when supporting a coworker going through a difficult time, working closely with a team to achieve a challenging goal, or watching a manager handle layoffs with humanity and compassion.

For me, spirituality means getting out of my own head and feeling emotionally and physically connected to something outside myself. I try to stave off my anxiety long enough to find stillness, which helps me discern what I can and can't control. I focus on something shared—a common good or a common experience—that doesn't preference my own needs and wants. My decisions are grounded in my values and a larger purpose in life. I acknowledge that my writing this chapter is from this belief, which continues to evolve. My view is that spirituality is a more common experience than any one particular religion, and I focus on what may be most useful for managing challenging work dilemmas, which is the point of this book.

I also acknowledge that others have different viewpoints and might write a different book. Someone whose practices are embedded in a particular religion might experience God. Someone else might experience spirituality as the interconnection of mind, body, and spirit. What's most important is what spirituality means to each of us in our everyday lives.

When we experience spirituality, we might focus less on job status, title, or salary and instead wonder about our purpose and happiness related to work. What impact could we have, and how can we enjoy our job? These questions lead some to find a vocation, or a calling, for a particular career. Oscar, an actor, says, "I'm an artist. That's what I do." He turns down jobs that don't feel connected to his core purpose and won't bring him joy, and he's lucky to find enough work to meet his financial needs.

When Naya, a personal trainer, considered how much her job paid, even with a potential promotion, she realized it wasn't much more than she would pay for day care. Instead, she quit to be a full-time mom. As she said, "Maybe this is what I should be doing now, anyway." She put the situation in perspective.

Connection

We might consider the spirit as what happens between people. At work, people can feel spiritual connections to coworkers, just as people in recovery feel connected to others in Twelve Step or other programs. Of course, the workplace has limitations, and we're cautioned against connections that get *too* personal. But working with others offers an opportunity for connection that many of us long for, and difficult work situations offer opportunities for special connections, for example, during the regional blackout. In solidarity, Elizabeth and her team of bandits huddled together, ignoring work titles and functions to create a new, supportive space for each other.

Collaboration is an important dimension of character and is one manifestation of spirituality in the workplace. Collaboration means functioning as part of a team and understanding how people affect each other—and how, conversely, what affects one person might affect everyone on a team. Teams work toward common goals, striving to achieve a shared purpose outside themselves.

Transcendence

Step 11 asks us to pray and meditate to deepen our contact with something we might call "greater than, deeper than, or beyond ourselves."[1] Our connection to a larger universe helps us find meaning in our lives—we *transcend* ourselves and our situations. Although prayer and meditation take many forms, with either, the purpose is to feel more peaceful and more emotionally balanced, and to have a greater sense of belonging and clarity, which helps us cope during difficult times.

Put simply, prayer is communication; a baby's cry is a form of prayer.[2] In her book *Help, Thanks, Wow: The Three Essential Prayers*, Anne LaMott describes asking for help, expressing gratitude, and showing appreciation.[3] Earlier, you read that asking for help is an act of humility, and so are expressions of gratitude and appreciation. We see ourselves in perspective.

Although both prayer and meditation may involve words and mantras as well as silence and listening, some consider prayer as communicating with words and meditation as stillness and listening. With both, we may benefit most by avoiding making specific requests or expecting ideal outcomes.

Prayer and meditation practices overlap with mindfulness, the most popular practice in the workplace, discussed in the chapter on faith. Progressive organizations dedicate space and allow time for employees to pray or meditate. For most of us, we need to find our own space for a few minutes of stillness—the act of *being* instead of *doing*—away from the chaos and busyness of work. Yoga and other physical exercise can also help us transcend ourselves.

All these practices help us develop "wisdom to know the difference"—not only wisdom about what we can change but also about our own selves and reality. Everyone, but perhaps particularly those of us with addiction histories, has trouble distinguishing between their own distorted thinking and the bigger picture. Wisdom includes seeing larger patterns, balancing our own and others' well-being, considering a common good, and addressing important, challenging questions.[4] At work, we use wisdom to practice good judgment and make good decisions.

Self-Absorption: Too Little Spiritual Awareness

Ivan, an experienced electrician, had trouble with his manager and the work. He wrote accusatory emails during the day and left long, rambling phone messages in the middle of the night. His manager suspected trouble with alcohol because he drank a case of beer at an after-work party. Regardless, Ivan got fired. For the next three years, he called his manager to offer help during busy times. In his messages, he said, "I can help out if you need me. Of course, it would be on my terms." Ivan could not see the situation from his manager's perspective. He would never get hired back.

Words related to too much focus on the self have subtle differences. To be *selfish* is to make decisions that benefit us or give us an advantage without regard to others.[5] A selfish person takes the best vacation slots and is uncompromising. To be *self-centered* is to be concerned only with what we want and what interests us. We don't consider outside factors.[6] To be *self-conscious* is to have a heightened sense of ourselves, possibly believing that people are more attuned to us than they are and causing discomfort in social situations.[7] A self-conscious person may fail to participate in meetings and be overly concerned with their appearance at work. A *self-absorbed* person is preoccupied or obsessed with themselves.[8]

With an intense focus on ourselves, we may have a "disproportionate reaction," a sign that we're taking things personally.[9] For example, we get angry about a schedule change, believing it was intended to inconvenience us, when the purpose was to accommodate a customer. Some of us are prickly. We may be easily offended and, as a result, miss out on a sense of belonging.

These afflictions are born out of low self-esteem.[10] As we hear in recovery meetings, some of us are "egomaniacs with an inferiority complex." We feel inferior to others, while still being egotistical, or overly focused on ourselves. Psychologists call this an ontological addiction, or an addiction to the self. People see themselves as apart from others rather than feeling interdependent or interconnected in a healthy way.[11]

Without emotional sobriety, we may be too dependent on others, seeking approval yet not getting what we need. Twelve Step programs offer spirituality as the solution: to find something more consistent and permanent to help us feel whole, connected, and accepted. As we gain spiritual awareness, we start seeing and experiencing our lives and connections to others from multiple perspectives, which gives us a more balanced understanding of ourselves. We might call this spiritual self-awareness—seeing ourselves accurately in relation to others.

Fundamentalism: Too Much Spiritual Awareness

When I was managing people, I gave an employee a low performance review because she often submitted work late and incomplete. My manager challenged me by asking what value she had to the company. The answer was easy. Her experience working at a client organization gave her good credibility with our clients. The truth is that I was threatened by her technical knowledge, which far surpassed mine. Controlling the details of her work was something I knew how to do. Once I saw the bigger picture, I gladly changed her review, although I still coached her to complete work on time.

Feeling self-conscious, I took a fundamentalist approach to the review. Fundamentalism is a "strict or literal adherence to a set of basic principles,"[12] in this case, checking off boxes on the review without seeing larger connections.

Some of us avoided Twelve Step programs because of religious experiences that felt fundamentalist. Some of us complain about "old timers" in the program who are rigid about the steps or principles. At work, we face similar ideas about how things "should be" or "have always been done." We saw this rigidity in other chapters of this book. Just as the self-righteous accepts no moral failings and the perfectionist accepts no flaws, the fundamentalist accepts no deviation from the rules.

The fundamentalist follows one set of rules—theirs. With no room for negotiation (or common sense), they don't consider others' needs, feelings, or ideas. The rules are the rules regardless of the situation. With this attitude, Elizabeth wouldn't have led the group into the company store—that's stealing!

Fundamentalists also might expect everyone to do their job in exactly the same way. But autonomy improves employees' satisfaction, performance, and motivation, so leaders and coworkers should avoid too many restrictions on how to perform a task.[13] Someone may need an accommodation, have a better idea, or simply want to work differently for the same or better results.

The Narrow Ridge of Spiritual Awareness

We balance our own needs with a larger perspective as we find our way on the narrow ridge of spiritual awareness. Expectations could set us up for disappointment and conflict, while managing through conflict and engaging in conversation are better ways to improve our working relationships.

Expectations

Expectations for ourselves serve a purpose. They clarify our standards, motivate us to achieve goals, and hold us accountable. Clear expectations for others communicate what we need from them and help us draw boundaries.

But setting expectations can set us up for disappointment and may be "resentments under construction."[14] The core of emotional dependency is relying on others to abide by our expectations. When people don't comply, we might feel hurt, sad, or angry. Wanting them to conform to our expectations is a way of controlling others. Instead, we return to concepts of willingness and acceptance. People do what they do; they have their own needs and expectations. We put our expectations aside and "let them," as discussed in the chapter on willingness.

One example at work is expecting fairness. The workplace is inherently unfair. Hiring requirements for degrees that aren't used, promotions that favor time over competence, wage disparities, and family-unfriendly schedules all benefit some people more than others. Working to change these systems takes courage, as discussed earlier, and can be a great, generative service. But simply railing against what doesn't work for us personally is futile.

In his book about emotional sobriety, Allen Berger suggests reframing "unfair" to "unfortunate" to better define and accept the situation.[15] Matthew won an industry award but received no recognition from management, not even an email. He felt resentful. Instead, he might have seen the situation as unfortunate. Maybe his management simply wasn't competent at giving positive feedback. What's also unfortunate is that Matthew set himself up for disappointment; he could find more reliable and consistent ways to get his emotional needs met. Matthew could reinforce his accomplishment by thanking the organization for the award and the person who nominated him. He could tell a friend about it or ask his family for time to talk about it. He can focus on his own gratitude for the recognition instead of seeking yet more external recognition.

Conflict

Often, expectations lead to conflicts, which can be painful but provide good practice for spiritual awareness—balancing our own needs and perspectives with a larger view. At work, we typically experience three types of conflicts, and they aren't all bad. Task conflicts are about the work itself. Different ideas or expectations about how work is assigned, how resources are allocated, and what procedures are used can improve outcomes. Relationship conflicts arise from personality differences, which can overshadow more productive task conflicts. Values conflicts refer to differences in politics, morals, identities, status, or security. These values may run deep—for example, avoiding a customer because of cultural differences—and are too often ignored.[16]

One approach to task conflicts is to think of them as team rather than individual problems. Instead of blaming one person, what are the factors causing the problem? Are roles and responsibilities clear? What training or information is needed? What's behind the conflict? Are deeper relationships or values differences at play?

Relationship and values conflicts may be tempered by getting to know each other and finding appreciation in our differences. Also, focusing on similarities instead of differences can help, but some conflicts linger and require a separate conversation.

When preparing to have a difficult conversation about a conflict, ask yourself a few questions. What assumptions do you have about this situation or about the other person? What could be the reasons for the behavior from the other person's perspective; in other words, could you be wrong about your interpretations? How might your emotions and your history contribute to the situation? Be careful about blaming others without examining your own responsibility, as we learn by taking the steps. Finally, how do you think the person might respond? Prepare for different reactions.[17]

Tired of one-word answers and grunts instead of morning hellos from her coworker, Tanya tried to discuss the tension between them. They had a good conversation, and her coworker admitted to being prone to holding grudges. Turns out, she was still upset about an incident between them months earlier. Tanya apologized—again—and things were a little better for a while, but the tension continued. She considered getting mediation help but decided to let it go. She couldn't control her coworker's resentment, so she worked on her own behavior and reactions and did her best not to let her coworker's hostility affect her mood, her work, or her self-esteem. Uncertainty about how, or whether, a conflict will resolve doesn't mean we have to live with constant anxiety over it.

Beyond mere tolerance of others, we work toward appreciating others. We see our differences not as annoyances we accommodate or as burdens we suffer but as ways to achieve greater understanding. We hear in recovery that a finger pointed at someone else leaves three pointed back at us. As people say, it's "another f---ing growth opportunity" to address something we avoided in the past.

Dialogue

As we work to resolve conflicts, we seek to understand others—and ourselves. In the best situations, we might even change our thinking as a result of our working and talking with others. We strive for dialogue—a "relationship-centered communication process that is sensitive to what happens to both self and other."[18] Our goal is to find that spiritual space between ourselves and another person, which is about neither of us but about something outside both of us that we discover together. Martin Buber called this space the narrow ridge because it's where we navigate our own perspectives as well as larger views—the subjective and the objective.[19]

Perhaps the least productive interpersonal communication style at work is *debate*, during which one side wins and the other loses. We attend only to ideas and ignore the whole person, looking for weaknesses in logic so we can be right. *Discussion* is better, but still focuses on content instead of feelings, and the goal is to persuade the other. In *dialogue*, we listen without judgment, explore feelings, find places we agree, create new meaning, and maybe change our own thinking. To build relationships, we allow ourselves to be more emotionally involved, value each other as whole people, and commit to the other's well-being.

Step 10 shows us how we can continually improve, and Step 11 deepens our tools for connection. When we got sober, we didn't know how our personal or professional relationships would change. We stay open, curious, and hopeful that we'll find a way forward even if we don't get the answers we thought we wanted. As Buber observed, "all journeys have secret destinations of which the traveler is unaware."[20]

Closing Thoughts

In active addiction, we may have spent years indulging thoughts of ourselves: how we had been wronged and how others failed us. To get sober, we may have prided ourselves on our independence—"white knuckling it" without any help or support. Spiritual awareness is an invitation to get out of our own distorted thinking to find connection outside ourselves.

The Latin *spiritualis* is "pertaining to breath, breathing, wind, or air."[21] With spiritual awareness, we emerge from ourselves to find what connects all beings, like the air we breathe. This puts us in a frame of mind to be of service to others, which is the last of the Twelve Steps.

Reflection Questions

1. What does spiritual awareness mean to you?
2. In what ways do you feel connected to people at work? How do these connections help you get outside of your own thinking?
3. When have you avoided an impulsive reaction at work? How were you able to choose a response after transcending your own situation and thinking?
4. When have you been selfish, self-centered, self-conscious, or self-absorbed at work? How did your actions affect others?
5. Identify a few expectations that may be causing you disappointment at work. How can you see the situation from other perspectives?
6. Describe a work conflict that you resolved well. What did you and the other person do to work through it?
7. Think about a work situation you can use to practice moving from debate to dialogue. How could this approach improve your relationship?

CHAPTER 12

Service

Chapter Overview

The last step in the Twelve Step program is about providing service to others, also useful at work. With a generous, grateful attitude, we find ways to help others and elevate their work. When we offer service, we don't expect anything in return, although we do receive benefits. To avoid suffocating ourselves or others, we balance how much we give and how much we take to preserve our own dignity and maintain healthy well-being.

Marcus's Dilemma

As we progress in recovery, we want to be of service to others—to "practice these principles in all our affairs," as Step 12 suggests. Here's Marcus's story:

> I was sober for seven years and worked for the bank for three. I saw a bunch of employee resource groups for different affiliations and thought it would be good to start one for people in recovery.
>
> This was a tough decision for me. I was really worried about being identified as a "drug addict" at work. I approached a couple of friends who are also in recovery, and we decided it was worth the risk to start something together. We got HR approval and went ahead!
>
> The group is great. We talk about things recovery related and not. One benefit I hadn't thought of was meeting people from different parts of the bank. If I have any work problem, I have a network of people I can call on. Also, we convinced the annual

picnic organizers not to serve alcohol. If people want it, they can bring their own.

I hadn't thought about "carrying the message" at work. But I'm glad I'm able to do that.

At meetings, we hear people say they are "gratefully recovering," meaning that their history of addiction gave them new opportunities. One of those opportunities is service.

Service at Work

Step 12 frames our service work as a result of a spiritual awakening, however we define it. Organizations function best when employees are generous, demonstrate gratitude, and elevate others. Our service can extend far beyond ourselves—to our workgroups, across an industry, and to future generations.

Spiritual Awakening

Step 12 encourages us to "carry this message" and "to practice these principles in all our affairs." Self-supporting and run by volunteers, all Twelve Step programs rely on the service of their members. In a broad sense, work environments also rely on service—for employees to follow through on commitments.

The first part of Step 12 is important too: "Having had a spiritual awakening as the result of these Steps." Like a higher power and spirituality, people define what a spiritual awakening means to them. Unlikely a flash of lightning or a vision of God, an awakening is more typically a gradual realization, like finding new strength or seeing clearly for the first time the possibility for a new approach to life. Bill W. wrote about his transformation:

> In the wake of my spiritual experience, there came a vision of a society of alcoholics, each identifying with and transmitting his experience to the next—chain style. If each sufferer were to carry the news of the scientific hopelessness of alcoholism to each new

prospect, he might be able to lay every newcomer wide open to a transforming spiritual experience. This concept proved to be the foundation of such success as AA has since achieved.[1]

After working a recovery program and applying the principles, we gladly provide service to others, as Marcus did by starting a recovery group at work.

Years before my recovery, I heard someone say, "You may feel like you're bothering me when you ask me to do something, but it's the opposite. I'm glad when you call. I want to help." At the time, I didn't get it at all, but today, I feel the same way. My focus shifted away from myself, and I experienced a sense of community and purpose that were new for me. In active addiction, I couldn't see beyond my own needs. Now I see my place in the universe, which gives me peace because my individual circumstances have become much less important, and my effort to have a positive impact on others much more important.

Generosity

Whether explicit or implicit, almost every job requires service. A customer service representative, a health care professional, an attorney, a mechanic—they all give something of their time or skills to provide clients, patients, or customers needing help. HR representatives, accountants, and security officers provide service to coworkers within the organization.

In any job, we can give just enough to meet the minimum expectations of our position description, or we can bring a generous spirit to our work. We practice workplace civility—being polite and respectful—but we offer even more. Defined as "the virtue of giving good things to others freely and abundantly,"[2] generosity means extending ourselves for others' well-being. We extend what we learn about service in recovery to our work. A security officer may spend extra time with an employee who feels unsafe by listening to their concerns, checking locks and stairwells, reassuring them, and checking in on them later in the day. The officer is patient and kind and cares for the employee without causing more harm.

As we hear in the rooms of recovery, "If you want to keep it, you have to give it away." We keep our sobriety by helping others, which, in turn, strengthens our recovery. Some sponsors joke that they have a 100 percent success rate with sponsees, meaning the sponsor has stayed sober. Being generous brings other personal rewards, for example, improved psychological well-being and happiness and, at work, more work satisfaction and less burnout.[3]

To be generous, we call on our humility, our compassion, and our spiritual awareness to focus on others instead of ourselves. Ganesh started a lending circle at work to help his coworkers cover emergency payments, fund investments, and build credit. Each person contributes to a pool of money that people take turns tapping into and paying back over time—interest free. Grateful to be in recovery and financially stable, Ganesh wanted to support others who need a boost.

Gratitude

"An attitude of gratitude" is another common Twelve Step saying. Gratitude is a mindset, but of course, gratitude is also being thankful and feeling joy after receiving a tangible or intangible gift.

The benefits of gratitude are well documented. At work, gratitude may lead to greater profitability, higher productivity, better customer satisfaction ratings, lower turnover, fewer accidents, and less theft.[4] In our personal lives, particularly with long-term practice, gratitude improves emotional and social well-being, for example, self-awareness, self-regulation, resilience, sense of belonging, and healthy relationships.[5] Gratitude also may decrease depression and anxiety and improve health outcomes, although research as of now is mixed.[6] Maybe the best benefit is that gratitude likely primes us to be more generous.[7] Feeling grateful for help when we're overwhelmed with a task reminds and inspires us to help others in similar situations—to pay it forward.

Like all character dimensions, gratitude is cultivated through practice. I heard someone say he wasn't "getting the joy and gratitude" he saw others have in recovery programs. But gratitude is something we give, not something we get. Popular methods for developing a gratitude practice are writing gratitude lists and keeping gratitude journals. We can send letters, emails, texts, or direct messages to people we appreciate. Or, as part of our Step 10 inventory, we can identify positive aspects of our day, ourselves, our work, and those around us.

A friend in recovery says that when he feels at his lowest point, the only thing that helps is gratitude. He says it's like a balloon: "I grab hold, and it lifts me out just a little bit."

Recognition

In the chapter on humility, we talked about making space for others. When we demonstrate gratitude, we go beyond making space to affirm and recognize others' work. As we get less self-absorbed, we focus on elevating others. We know the value of recognition at recovery meetings. We thank each other after shares, say each other's name, and applaud any time in sobriety.

Although workplaces can be dismal places, anyone can make another person feel better with a positive message. When employees feel recognized—when others express gratitude for their work—they feel happier, more motivated, and more competent.[8]

Some people avoid recognizing others because they worry about saying or writing something awkward. We also underestimate the positive effect a genuine note of thanks will have on the receiver.[9] Our recovery work is to get past this self-consciousness to provide service to someone else. Positive messages are best received when they're sent quickly after an event, are sincere, are brief, and state specifically what the person did and the positive impact on others.[10]

Impact

Although small acts of service are still appreciated, larger acts can have enormous impacts. Waiting with a coworker for a ride or buying them a cup of coffee are examples of practicing the principle of service. As discussed in the chapter on compassion, often our presence and attention are enough.

But other acts of service pull us away from our day-to-day work to see bigger problems to solve. While working as a hotel restaurant server,

Marianne convinced management to work with local nonprofits that redistribute food. She was able to save the company money on waste removal and get meals to families who needed them. Over time, more restaurants in the area adopted the program, which created a ripple effect to reduce environmental waste and food insecurity.

What starts small affects people in future generations. Lending circles like the one Ganesh started help people pay off debt, start a small business, and buy a car. What improves financial security in the short term could create wealth in the long term.

Ingratitude: Too Little Service

In active addiction, some of us were ungrateful, expecting more than we were willing or able to give. We may have been greedy, more focused on our rights than our responsibilities, or believing we deserved special treatment.

Selfish and self-centered, entitled workers make unreasonable demands. They may be unwilling to do anything outside their job description, fail to follow instructions, or expect more rewards for less work.[11] Feeling this way leads to frustration and disappointment; again, our expectations set us up and set us apart from others. Thinking we deserve more can leave us angry and resentful—ungrateful.

For their part, managers can be stingy, even when work deserves praise and recognition. Employees often don't get the positive feedback they want and leave their job because they don't feel valued. Hearing only criticism can be demoralizing and may discourage people from making any changes at all.

Sometimes, recognition is fake. When Catherine was invited out for coffee on the weekend by her coworker, Anita, she was excited to go, thinking she might make a new friend. After a half-hour of chit-chat, Anita's demeanor changed: "Well, I wanted to ask for your expertise on something." She proceeded to talk about reorganizing her office. Catherine, a professional organizer, was taken aback. This is the kind of work she would typically get paid for. Later, Catherine said, "It was strange because we worked together for a year before that, and Anita was always cool to me. Suddenly, she acted like my best friend."

We may have a difficult time distinguishing niceness from deceit. The word nice has negative connotations for good reason: It sounds demeaning, for example, when we tell a child to "be nice" to get them to pet a dog gently. The nice coworker is sweet as pie, and their acts are *ingratiating*, meaning they flatter us and demand flattery in return—just for being nice.[12]

After seeing this pattern, we don't trust the coworker; we see the behavior as manipulative, as Catherine did. On the face of it, Anita was nice, inviting Catherine out for coffee, but she had ulterior motives. These actions aren't real acts of service; they serve the giver more than the receiver, which also may be the case when we overdo service, which we explore next.

Suffocation: Too Much Service

Just as damaging as ingratitude is suffocating people with our good deeds. Step 12 suggests that we "*try* to carry the message"; the message is not always wanted or needed. At recovery meetings, we greet newcomers but don't smother them. Too much service can be condescending, as though we don't believe someone can be self-sufficient. We create dependence and maybe, eventually, resentment.

Even people in service jobs can be over the top. They may mean well, but hair stylists who stand too close, take too long, or ask too many questions can annoy customers. They don't adjust according to subtle, or direct, feedback they receive.

In other cases, our intentions are obviously self-serving. The coworker who waits in the parking lot with an umbrella to run into a love interest and escort them to the building doesn't have pure intentions. A coworker may use service as a disguise to manipulate, bully, or harass. Henri offered to edit a proposal but rewrote the entire document in his own style and voice. He gave no explanation or feedback to the writer, who did not want or appreciate that kind of help.

We also can suffocate ourselves with service. When we allow service to negatively impact our health, safety, financial security, or relationships, it's time to question how much is too much. In recovery programs, we're mindful to manage our commitments to allow time and space for our own recovery. Amari took the initiative to celebrate employees' birthdays, decorating the office and distributing cards for everyone to sign. After a few months, he resented the time it took and didn't want to be known as the department party planner. He cut back to monthly gatherings with a cake—finding a balance.

The Narrow Ridge of Service

Service can be reciprocal. Although we act without expecting anything in return, we do benefit from service. We find balance between giving and taking to serve others, yet advance, rather than stifle, our own careers.

Reciprocity

Of course, people who give also get something in return. There's nothing wrong with feeling good about being of service, getting thanked, or receiving unexpected benefits. Marcus relied on his work friends to support the employee resource group, and he found a network for help on the job that he didn't expect.

Although people may be hesitant, as we learn in recovery, there's also nothing wrong with asking for and receiving help. We're socialized toward gratitude; receiving help reminds us that we should reciprocate.[13] At the end of Twelve Step meetings, we say, "Keep coming back." This serves members who want to stay clear of their addictive substance or behavior—and, in turn, it makes our meetings continue.

Reciprocity is how business operates. In addition to the obvious payment for service, reciprocity is a powerful tool of persuasion.[14] You may have received a bonus for referring a new employee or a 10 percent discount for giving a retail company your email. Giving and receiving creates an expected pattern of behavior.

Give and Take

How do we find the balance of giving, so we're generous but not suffocating others or sabotaging our career? In his book *Give and Take*,

Adam Grant describes "givers" and "takers." Givers value helpfulness, responsibility, social justice, and compassion. They tip the benefit balance in others' favor. Takers, who we might consider ungrateful and giving too little service, value wealth, power, pleasure, and winning. They believe in competition—winners and losers.[15]

Surprisingly, givers end up at both the top and the bottom of the success ladder. They are both the most and least productive engineers and receive both the highest and lowest grades in medical school. The difference is in how and how much they give. The most successful givers are also willing to receive. Although they give without expectation, they do get more than they give in the long run. They also have a stopping point, unlike the least successful givers, who are "too trusting, too caring, and too willing to sacrifice their own interests for the benefit of others."[16]

In recovery, we learn not to be taken advantage of—not to get entangled with people who could jeopardize our sobriety. At work, we're not saps. We want to be responsible, trusted, helpful, and yet respected.

Greater Impact

To have the greatest impact, we put more of ourselves into service work. As we have more time in recovery and feel more confident with ourselves and in our careers, we may be able to take more risks and expand our reach.

When a young woman came to the emergency room, the doctor on call couldn't identify what was wrong. He sent her home with some medication, but she died in the middle of the night of an illness that could not have been identified given the information they had at the time. Of course, the family was devastated, and so was the doctor. His service was sitting with the family, on one knee, explaining the decision they made, neither diminishing their feelings nor further enraging them. With his time and presence, the family was able to grieve instead of rage. His was an act both small and large, both simple and enormously complex, but with far-reaching impact.

As another example, a group of experts in food production—scientists, food-handling businesspeople, and government officials—

from more than 100 countries formed an international association to promote healthy, safe food. The members represent not their own organization but a larger, shared purpose: vetting food safety issues to improve practices and to protect companies and other parties from retaliatory, false claims. The association challenges members to advance global, long-term goals that, at times, may conflict with their individual organization's interests. For example, they set up a process for anonymous whistleblowers to report unsafe food conditions, even though some of their organizations may have engaged in these practices. Their commitment to address serious, global issues requires them to face controversy in their own workplace to serve bigger goals.

By working the steps, we gain self-awareness and perspective that allows us to initiate and accept such opportunities. We consider the risks and take more of them, knowing how service can extend beyond our recovery groups and workplaces to bring about significant change and greater impact.

Closing Thoughts

Recovery programs teach us the value of service, and we share that with our coworkers. We "practice these principles in all our affairs," including our work environment.

Having transcended ourselves to care for others, we find ways to create a supportive, generative workplace, where ideas and people can grow. The workplace doesn't have to be a toxic, competitive place. From any position in an organization, or if we work alone, we can demonstrate good character and be of service to others. Our gratitude and generosity create ripple effects that multiply the benefits of recovery in ways we may have never imagined.

Reflection Questions

1. At work, who do you consider generous with their time, attention, resources, or skills? How is this person perceived?

2. In what ways do you provide service at work? Consider how you generously offer your time, attention, resources, and skills.

3. How can you recognize or elevate others' work? Think of something small you can do.

4. Have you felt ungrateful at work? What was the situation, and how did you pull out of it? If you're still feeling that way, what change can you make either in your work or in your approach?

5. Was there a time at work when you provided too much service? What was the negative effect, and how did you adjust your time? Is this something you need to do now?

6. On balance, do you consider yourself more of a giver or more of a taker at work? Are you giving as well as receiving?

7. What could you do at work that could positively affect others? Think about both small acts of service that affect a few people and larger initiatives that could affect people in other organizations or across an industry.

Conclusion

Twelve Step programs offer a new way of living, including a fresh approach to work and career challenges. In recovery, we want what anyone wants: to feel at peace and productive. We want to start our workday, if not with great enthusiasm, then at least with a determination to contribute and to do our best. We want to end our workday with satisfaction that we did the best we could and will do better tomorrow. No one wants to feel foreboding dread before work or relentless anxiety after, particularly if addictive substances and behaviors feel like the only solution.

The foundational principles explored in this book are tools to achieve that serenity. The principles are ancient and grounded in character—the sum of who we are. We practice the principles, not as common-sense abstractions, but as observable skills that anyone can develop with enough commitment. Our reward is deepening our recovery and improving our emotional sobriety, which allows us to handle situations in healthy and constructive ways. With this growth, we are no longer triggered and don't need our addictive substances or behaviors to cope.

Muddy and crowded at times, the workplace is a serious sandbox. With all its pressure and revolving cast of characters, we have no better place to practice strengthening our own character. The work before us can be overwhelming. But in our careers, as in our personal lives, we take it one step at a time and one day at a time.

The narrow ridge can be rocky. Every step takes courage. C.S. Lewis observed that "courage is not simply *one* of the virtues, but the form of every virtue at the testing point."[1] We are not honest or compassionate only when it's easy for us. Even when we face adversity, we still live true to our values and to the principles we learn in recovery. We avoid slipping into the extremes and, instead, learn to recognize the tipping points and act in moderation, something we couldn't do in active addiction. We become more stable as we discern what we can change and the many circumstances and people we cannot change and have to accept. We emerge as more resilient, adaptable, and agile.

Martin Buber's biographer, Maurice Friedman, explains his relevance to our work:

> Martin Buber's significance for us was not that he was a saint or even one to whom the life of dialogue came easily, but rather that he was a person who embodied the contradictions and ambiguities of modern existence and yet was able again and again to reach personal wholeness and integrity in faithful response to the persons and situations of his time.[2]

We face "contradictions and ambiguities" every day at work. Yet despite the uncertainty of a new boss, job, or system, we persevere. We know ourselves well enough to trust that we'll resist impulsive reactions we later regret. Instead, we humbly canvas the situation and intuitively assess others' needs so we can respond as wholly integrated people. We have become wise.

We use good judgment and make good decisions that consider how others will be affected. We act with integrity and, most times, choose a course that has a more positive impact on others than on ourselves. We do this because we genuinely want what's best for others.

We're not perfect at work, just as we're not perfect at home. Sometimes we push too hard or not hard enough. We miss a few offenses and invent a few that weren't intended. But we keep ourselves in check and apologize when we're wrong. We always strive to do better, and we are better.

Our work on ourselves has ripple effects. Having the experience of recovery provides gifts that must be passed along at work. Who better to remedy a toxic workplace that triggers relapse and worse? When we are honest about our addiction history during a job interview, our employer takes a chance on us and, seeing the good results, takes a chance on others. When we are hopeful about our start-up, we attract new customers, hire people, and create our own work community. When we have faith that, even if we lose our job, we'll be OK, we relieve our family's stress, and show our children how to manage through adversity.

At some point, we look back on our careers and are amazed at what we accomplished—not the money, status, or prestige but the impact we had on others' lives, the legacy we leave from the small acts of compassion to the large acts of service. At some point, our careers became no longer about us but about spiritual connections outside of us. We did far more than stay sober at work. We walked the narrow ridge and recovered at work.

Notes

Introduction

1. Taub, *God of Our Understanding,* 7–11.
2. Gaba, "All or Nothing Thinking."
3. Friedman, *Encounter on the Narrow Ridge,* 43–44.
4. Friedman.
5. Online Etymology Dictionary, "recover."
6. Alcoholics Anonymous World Services, *Alcoholics Anonymous,* 83–84.
7. Friedman, *Encounter on the Narrow Ridge,* 43–44.
8. Arnett, *Communication and Community,* 159–60.
9. Bill, *Twelve Steps and Twelve Traditions,* 15.
10. Peterson and Seligman, *Character Strengths and Virtues,* 10.
11. Pittman, *Practice These Principles,* xi.
12. Seijts, Crossan, and Carleton, "Embedding Leader Character," 30.
13. Kraut, "Aristotle's Ethics."
14. Hazelden Betty Ford Foundation, "Boundaries in Addiction Recovery."
15. Alcoholics Anonymous World Services, *Alcoholics Anonymous,* 59–60. The Twelve Steps are adapted with permission of Alcoholics Anonymous World Services, Inc.
16. Bill, *AA Grapevine,* 3.
17. Adult Children of Alcoholics and Dysfunctional Families, "Secular ACA Serenity Prayer."

Chapter 1

1. Alcoholics Anonymous, "Twelve Questions."
2. Intel, "Powerless to Purpose."
3. Bill, *Twelve Steps and Twelve Traditions,* 32 and 54.
4. *Alcoholics Anonymous,* xiv.
5. Bill, *Twelve Steps and Twelve Traditions,* 114.
6. Chamorro-Premuzic, "How and Why We Lie."

7. Bill, *Twelve Steps and Twelve Traditions*, 24.

8. Britannica, "Lawrence Kohlberg's Stages."

9. Schwarz, "The 'Sandwich Approach.'"

10. French and Holden, "Positive Organizational Behavior," 209.

11. Bok, *Lying*, 58.

12. Levine and Schweitzer, "Are Liars Ethical?," 108.

13. Troup and Marinchak, "Niceness, Flattery, and Deceit," 66.

14. Newman, *Business Communication and Character*, 6–18.

15. Cai and Wu, "Dark Side of White Lies," 1–14.

16. Alcoholics Anonymous, "How It Works."

Chapter 2

1. Alcoholics Anonymous, "What to Expect."

2. Lopez, "Science of Hope."

3. Samuel, "Why Cornel West Is Hopeful."

4. Samuel.

5. Plante, "Role of Personal Hope," 88.

6. Snyder, "Hope Theory," 249–275.

7. Lopez, "The Science of Hope."

8. Snyder, "Hope Theory," 252.

9. Peterson and Seligman, *Character Strengths and Virtues*, 569.

10. Scioli et al., "Hope: Its Nature," 82.

11. Shanahan et al., "Does Despair Really Kill?" 855.

12. Shanahan et al., 854.

13. Shanahan et al., 854–858.

14. Cleveland Clinic, "HALT."

15. Peterson and Seligman, *Character Strengths and Virtues*, 571.

16. Chignell, "Empowering Ideas."

17. *Alcoholics Anonymous*, 44.

18. Chignell, "Hope Versus Optimism."

19. Chignell, "Empowering Ideas."

20. Chignell.

21. West, "Those who have never."

Chapter 3

1. Online Etymology Dictionary, "confidence."
2. Alcoholics Anonymous General Service Office, "Origins of the Serenity Prayer."
3. Griffin, *One Breath at a Time*, 51.
4. Griffin, 21.
5. Achor and Gielan, "The Busier You Are."
6. Achor and Gielan.
7. Basso et al., "Brief, Daily Meditation," 215.
8. Alcoholics Anonymous General Service Office, "Origins of the Serenity Prayer."
9. Schulz, *Peanuts*.
10. Mayo, *Bartlett's Unfamiliar Quotations*, 331.
11. Benson, "Cognitive Bias Cheat Sheet."
12. Knox, "After I was convicted."
13. Knox.
14. Carelton et al., "Increasing Intolerance," 121–136.
15. Molinsky, "If You're Not Outside."
16. Bill, *Twelve Steps and Twelve Traditions*, 36–38.
17. Mashal et al., "Brief Worry Reappraisal Paradigm," 216–228.
18. Newman, "How to Feel Confident."
19. Marijuana Anonymous World Services, *Life with Hope*, 61–62.
20. Alcoholics Anonymous General Service Office, "Origins of the Serenity Prayer."

Chapter 4

1. Alcoholics Anonymous General Service Office, "Origins of the Serenity Prayer."
2. Kidder, *Moral Courage*, 7.
3. 12Step.org, "Fourth Step Inventory."
4. *Alcoholics Anonymous*, 64–68.
5. *Alcoholics Anonymous*, 67.
6. Newman, "Motivations and Risks."
7. Narcotics Anonymous, "Just for Today."

8. Hirschman, *Exit, Voice, and Loyalty*, 21–29.

9. Worline, "Courage in Organizations."

10. Kitroeff, Gelles, and Nicas, "Boeing 737."

11. McGregor, "Maya Angelou on Leadership."

12. Taitz, "Honest Communication."

13. Kidder, *Moral Courage*, 130–138.

14. Blest, "Leaked Amazon Memo."

15. Blest.

16. Ji, "Blowing the Whistle."

17. Nakken, *Finding Your Moral Compass*, 115.

18. Bill, *Twelve Steps and Twelve Traditions*, 7–8.

Chapter 5

1. Peterson and Seligman, *Character Strengths and Virtues*, 249–50.

2. Online Etymology Dictionary, "integrity."

3. Cha et al., "Being Your True Self," 634.

4. Wood et al., "The Authentic Personality," 385–399.

5. Buote, "Most Employees Feel Authentic."

6. Van den Bosch and Taris, "Authenticity at Work," 1–18.

7. Simons, *The Integrity Dividend*, 5.

8. Bill, *Twelve Steps and Twelve Traditions*, 69.

9. Ibarra, "The Authenticity Paradox."

10. Cialdini and Goldstein, "Science and Practice of Persuasion," 45.

11. Literary Devices, "To Thine Own Self."

12. *AA Grapevine*, "The Clip Sheet."

13. Brené Brown, "Dare to Lead."

Chapter 6

1. Sandy, "'Drop the Rock' Talk."

2. Bill, Todd, and Sara, *Drop the Rock*, x.

3. Bill, Todd, and Sara, xi.

4. Bill, *Twelve Steps and Twelve Traditions*, 3–4.

5. Bill, Todd, and Sara, *Drop the Rock*, 2.

6. Al-Anon's Family Groups, "Al-Anon's Three Cs."

7. Robbins, "The 'Let Them Theory.'"

8. Reisinger and Fetterer, "Forget Flexibility."

9. Cohen, "Promoting Ethical Judgment," 513–523.

10. Taub, *God of Our Understanding*, 159.

11. George, "By accepting both."

12. From Adler. See Watts and Trusty, "Using Imaginary Team Members."

13. Cuddy, "Your Body Language."

14. Coles, Larsen, and Lench, "A Meta-Analysis," 644–645.

15. Coles, Larsen, and Lench.

16. Elsesser, "The Debate on Power Posing."

17. Vakola, "The Reasons," 203.

18. Elving, "The Role of Communication," 129–138.

19. Vakola, "The Reasons," 213.

20. Griffin, *One Breath at a Time*, 137.

21. Taub, *God of Our Understanding*, 153.

Chapter 7

1. Warren, *Purpose Driven Life*, 149.

2. Hamilton, "Non-Stop."

3. Rego et al., "Leader Humility."

4. Peterson and Seligman, *Character Strengths and Virtues,* 431–438.

5. DeSteno, *Emotional Success*, 115–140.

6. Leary et al., "Cognitive and Interpersonal Features," 793–813.

7. Allyn, "Elizabeth Holmes Trial."

8. Newman, *Business Communication and Character*, 269.

9. SHRM, "What Should an Employer Tell."

10. Arnett, *Communication and Community*, 32.

11. Kanter, "Managing Yourself."

12. Bill, *Twelve Steps and Twelve Traditions*, 70.

Chapter 8

1. Dutton, Workman, and Hardin, "Compassion at Work," 277–304; Worline and Dutton, *Awakening Compassion at Work*, 5.

2. Pommier, Neff, and Tóth-Király, "Development and Validation," 23.

3. Goetz, Keltner, and Simon-Thomas, "Compassion," 355–358.

4. Sahi et al., "One Size," 1522–1535.

5. Alcoholics Anonymous, "What to Expect."

6. Sahi et al., "One Size," 1531.

7. Raes et al., "Construction and Factorial Validation," 250–251.

8. Raes et al., "Short Form," 251–252.

9. Neff, "Self-Compassion Guided Practices."

10. Palmer, "Stop Asking."

11. Kross, *Chatter*, 48–86.

12. Bill, *Twelve Steps and Twelve Traditions*, 184.

13. Lv et al., "Effects of Loving-Kindness," 1–18.

14. DeSteno, *Emotional Success*, 88–92 and 106–109.

15. Frankl, *Man's Search for Meaning*, 86.

16. Singer and Klimecki, "Empathy and Compassion," R875–R878.

17. Stellar et al., "Class and Compassion," 449–450.

18. Baez et al., "Men, Women."

19. Walker, *Art of Comforting*, 6–8.

20. DeSteno, *Emotional Success*, 102–103.

Chapter 9

1. Online Etymology Dictionary, "amend."

2. Brees, Sikora, and Ferris, "Workplace Accountabilities," 519.

3. Brees, Sikora, and Ferris, 520.

4. Cohen, "Promoting Ethical Judgment."

5. Hautala, "Amazon Adjusts."

6. Brees, Sikora, and Ferris, "Workplace Accountabilities," 521.

7. Schumann, "An Affirmed Self," 89–96.

8. Schumann and Dragotta, "Empathy as a Predictor," 896–909.

9. Nelson, Malkoc, and Shiv, "Emotions Know Best," 40–51.

10. Covington, *A Woman's Way*, 147–149.

11. Covington, 152.

12. Online Etymology Dictionary, "resent."

13. Rasmussen et al., "Meta-Analytic Connections," 515–534.

14. Rasmussen et al., 516.

15. Scott, *Radical Candor*, 22–42.

16. Bill, *Twelve Steps and Twelve Traditions*, 84.

17. *Alcoholics Anonymous*, 164.

Chapter 10

1. Holiday and Hanselman, *Lives of the Stoics*, xi.

2. Crossan et al., "Toward a Framework," 1001.

3. Southwick, Tsay, and Duckworth, "Grit at Work."

4. Eurich, "What Self-Awareness."

5. Lieberman, "Why You Procrastinate."

6. Uysal and Yilmaz, "Procrastination in the Workplace," 83–84.

7. Uysal and Yilmaz, 84–86.

8. Burnett and Evans, *Designing Your Life*, 41–55.

9. Pink, *Drive*, 101–130.

10. Pink, 131–146.

11. Coldwell, "Rise of Perfectionism."

12. Knight, "Manage Your Perfectionism."

13. Harari et al., "Is Perfect Good?," 1121–1144.

14. Bill, *Twelve Steps and Twelve Traditions*, 91.

15. Burnett and Evans, xxxix

16. Burnett and Evans, xxvi.

17. Knight, "Manage Your Perfectionism."

18. Gragnano, Simbula, and Miglioretti, "Work-Life Balance," 907.

19. Workaholics Anonymous, "The Twenty Questions."

20. Duke, *Quit*, 27–32.

21. Duke, 115–127.

22. Carden and Wood, "Habit Formation," 117–119.

23. DePaul, "What Does It Take?"

Chapter 11

1. Covington, *A Woman's Way*, 185.

2. Ulanov and Ulanov, *Primary Speech*, 2.

3. Lamott, *Help, Thanks, Wow*, 182.

4. Peterson and Seligman, *Character Strengths and Virtues*, 182.

5. Merriam-Webster, "selfish."

6. Merriam-Webster, "self-centered."

7. Merriam-Webster, "self-conscious."

8. Merriam-Webster, "self-absorbed."

9. Berger, *12 Essential Insights*, 109.

10. Berger, 110.

11. Van Gordon, "Why an Inferiority Complex."

12. Merriam-Webster, "fundamentalism."

13. Slemp et al., "Leader Autonomy Support," 719–720.

14. Berger, *12 Essential Insights*, 281.

15. Berger, 166.

16. Shonk, "3 Types of Conflict."

17. Newman, "Preparing for Difficult Conversations."

18. Arnett, *Communication and Community*, 7.

19. Friedman, *Encounter on the Narrow Ridge*, 247.

20. Buber, *The Legend of the Baal-Shem*, 36.

21. Online Etymology Dictionary, "spirituality."

Chapter 12

1. Bill W. to Dr. Carl Gustav Jung.

2. Science of Generosity, "What Is Generosity?"

3. Allen, "Science of Generosity," 19–27.

4. Emmons, "Gratitude."

5. Jans-Beken et al., "Gratitude and Health," 1–40.

6. Jans-Beken et al., "Gratitude and Health"; Cregg and Cheavens, "Gratitude Interventions," 413–445; Boggiss et al., "Systematic Review," 36.

7. DeSteno, *Emotional Success*, 58–59.

8. Tessema, Ready, and Embaye, "Effects of Employee Recognition," 1–12.

9. Kumar and Epley, "Undervaluing Gratitude," 1423–1435.

10. Newman, *Business Communication and Character*, 196.

11. White, "Age of Entitlement."

12. Troup and Marinchak, "Niceness, Flattery, and Deceit," 69–71.

13. Peterson and Seligman, *Character Strengths and Virtues*, 556–557.

14. Cialdini and Goldstein, "Science of Persuasion," 40–50.

15. Grant, *Give and Take*, 4–5.

16. Grant, 7.

Conclusion

1. Lewis, "Screwtape Letters," 63.

2. Friedman, *Encounter on the Narrow Ridge,* x.

Bibliography

AA Grapevine. "The Clip Sheet: Excerpts from the Public Press." July 1947. https://www.aagrapevine.org/magazine/1947/jul/clip-sheet.

Achor, Shawn and Michelle Gielan. "The Busier You Are, the More You Need Mindfulness." *Harvard Business Review*, December 18, 2015. https://hbr.org/2015/12/the-busier-you-are-the-more-you-need-mindfulness.

Adult Children of Alcoholics and Dysfunctional Families. "Steps." Accessed April 17, 2024. https://adultchildren.org/literature/steps.

Al-Anon's Family Groups. "Al-Anon's Three Cs." Accessed December 19, 2023. https://al-anon.org/blog/al-anons-three-cs.

Alcoholics Anonymous General Service Office. "Origins of the Serenity Prayer: A Historical Paper." Accessed December 21, 2023. https://www.aa.org/sites/default/files/literature/assets/smf-129_en.pdf.

Alcoholics Anonymous World Services, Inc. *Alcoholics Anonymous*. 4th ed. New York: AA Grapevine, Inc., 2001.

Alcoholics Anonymous. "How It Works." Accessed March 6, 2024. https://www.aa.org/sites/default/files/literature/assets/p-10_howitworks.pdf.

———. "Twelve Questions Only You Can Answer." Accessed March 6, 2024. https://www.aa.org/self-assessment.

———. "What to Expect at an A.A. Meeting." Accessed March 6, 2024. https://www.aa.org/information-about-meetings.

Allen, Summer. "The Science of Generosity." White paper prepared for The John Templeton Foundation. The Greater Good Science Center at UC Berkeley. May 2018. https://ggsc.berkeley.edu/images/uploads/GGSC-JTF_White_Paper-Generosity-FINAL.pdf.

Allyn, Bobby. "The Elizabeth Holmes Trial Is Sparking a Gender Debate in Silicon Valley." *NPR*, September 24, 2021. https://www.npr.org/2021/09/24/1040353540/the-elizabeth-holmes-trial-is-sparking-a-gender-debate.

Arménio Rego et al. "Leader Humility and Team Performance: Exploring the Mediating Mechanisms of Team PsyCap and Task Allocation Effectiveness." *Journal of Management* 45, no. 3 (January 2017).

Arnett, Ronald C. *Communication and Community*. Carbondale and Edwardsville: Board of Trustees, Southern Illinois University, 1986.

B., Sandy. "'Drop the Rock' Talk by Sandy B (the famous 1976 AA Convention Talk)." YouTube. Accessed March 7, 2024. https://www.youtube.com/watch?v=b3odwo4T5oI.

Baez, Sandra, Daniel Flichtentrei, María Prats, Ricardo Mastandueno, Adolfo M. García, Marcelo Cetkovich, Agustín Ibáñez. "Men, Women. . .Who Cares? A Population-Based Study on Sex Differences and Gender Roles in Empathy and Moral Cognition." *PLoS ONE* 12, no. 6 (June 2017). http://journals. plos.org/plosone/article?id=10.1371/journal.pone.0179336.

Basso, Julia C., Alexandra McHale, Victoria Ende, Douglas J. Oberlin, and Wendy A. Suzuki. "Brief, Daily Meditation Enhances Attention, Memory, Mood, and Emotional Regulation in Non-Experienced Meditators." *Behavioural Brain Research* 356, no. 1 (January 2019): 208–220.

Benson, Buster. "Cognitive Bias Cheat Sheet." BetterHumans. September 1, 2016. https://betterhumans.pub/cognitive-bias-cheat-sheet-55a472476b18.

Berger, Allen. *12 Essential Insights for Emotional Sobriety*. Los Angeles: 4th Dimension Publishing, 2021.

Blest, Paul. "Leaked Amazon Memo Details Plan to Smear Fired Warehouse Organizer: 'He's Not Smart or Articulate.'" *Vice*, April 2, 2023. https://www. vice.com/en/article/5dm8bx/leaked-amazon-memo-details-plan-to-smear -fired-warehouse-organizer-hes-not-smart-or-articulate.

Boggiss, Anna L., Nathan S. Consedine, Jennifer M. Brenton-Peters, Paul L. Hofman, and Anna S. Serlachius. "A Systematic Review of Gratitude Interventions: Effects on Physical Health and Health Behaviors." *Journal of Psychosomatic Research* 135 (August 2020): 1–41. http://doi:10.1016/j. jpsychores.2020.110165.

Bok, Sissela. *Lying: Moral Choice in Public and Private Life*. New York: Vintage Books, 1999.

Brees, Jeremy R., David M. Sikora, and Gerald R. Ferris. "Workplace Accountabilities: Worthy Challenge or Potential Threat?" *Career Development International* 25, no. 5 (2020): 517–37. https://doi-org.proxy.library.cornell. edu/10.1108/CDI-10-2019-0257.

Britannica. "Lawrence Kohlberg's Stages of Moral Development." Accessed March 6, 2024. https://www.britannica.com/topic/reason.

Brown, Brené. "Dare to Lead List of Values." Accessed December 28, 2023. https://brenebrown.com/resources/dare-to-lead-list-of-values.

Buber, Martin. *The Legend of the Baal-Shem*. Translated by Maurice Friedman. New York: Harper & Brothers, 1955.

Buote, Vanessa. "Most Employees Feel Authentic at Work, But It Can Take a While." *Harvard Business Review*, May 11, 2016. https://hbr.org/2016/05/ most-employees-feel-authentic-at-work-but-it-can-take-a-while.

Burnett, Bill and Dave Evans. *Designing Your Life: How to Build a Well-Lived, Joyful Life*. New York: Alfred A. Knopf, 2018.

———. *The Designing Your Life Workbook: A Framework for Building a Life You Can Thrive In*, Workbook Ed. Clarkson Potter, 2018.

Cai, Shiyu and Song Wu. "Dark Side of White Lies: How Altruistic Lying Impacts Subsequent Self-Interested Lying." *Current Psychology* (May 2023): 1–14.

Carden, Lucas and Wendy Wood. "Habit Formation and Change." *Current Opinion in Behavioral Sciences* 20 (January 2018): 117–22. https://doi.org/10.1016/j.cobeha.2017.12.009.

Carelton, R. Nicholas, Gabrielle Desgagné, Rachel Krakauer, and Ryan Y Hong. "Increasing Intolerance of Uncertainty Over Time: The Potential Influence of Increasing Connectivity." *Cognitive Behavioral Therapy* 48, no. 2 (2019): 121–36. http://doi.org/10.1080/16506073.2018.1476580.

Cha, Sandra E., Patricia Faison Hewlin, Laura Morgan Roberts, Brooke R. Buckman, Hannes Leroy, Erica L. Steckler, Kathryn Ostermeier, and Danielle Cooper. "Being Your True Self at Work: Integrating the Fragmented Research on Authenticity in Organizations." *Academy of Management Annals* 13, no. 2 (July 2019): 633–71.

Chamorro-Premuzic, Tomas. "How and Why We Lie at Work." *Harvard Business Review*, January 2, 2015. https://hbr.org/2015/01/how-and-why-we-lie-at-work.

Chignell, Andrew. "Empowering Ideas: A Philosopher Talks About Bad Hope, Good Hope and Despair." We Roar. Center for Human Values. Princeton University. June 5, 2020. http://weroar.princeton.edu/20-empowering-ideas-a-philosopher-talks-about-bad-hope-good-hope-and-despair.

———. "Hope Versus Optimism—Andrew Chignell on Anna Deavere Smith." *Tell Me More.* KET. PBS. April 5, 2022. https://ket.org/program/tell-me-more-with-kelly-corrigan-13505/hope-versus-optimism-andrew-chignell-on-anna-deveare-smit.

Cialdini, Robert B. and Noah J. Goldstein. "The Science and Practice of Persuasion." *Cornell Hotel and Restaurant Administration Quarterly* 43, no 2 (2002): 40–50.

Cleveland Clinic. "HALT: Pay Attention to These Four Stressors on Your Recovery." May 24, 2022. https://health.clevelandclinic.org/halt-hungry-angry-lonely-tired.

Cohen, Stephen. "Promoting Ethical Judgment in an Organisational Context." *Journal of Business Ethics* 117, no. 3 (October 2013): 513–23.

Coldwell, Will. "The Rise of Perfectionism—and the Harm It's Doing Us All." *The Guardian*, June 4, 2023. https://www.theguardian.com/society/2023/jun/04/the-rise-of-perfectionism-and-the-harm-its-doing-us-all.

Coles, Nicholas Alvaro, Jeff T. Larsen, and Heather C. Lench. "A Meta-Analysis of the Facial Feedback Literature: Effects of Facial Feedback on Emotional Experience Are Small and Variable. *Psychological Bulletin 145, no. 6* (April 2019): 610–51. https://doi.org/10.1037/bul0000194.

Covington, Stephanie S. *A Woman's Way through the Twelve Steps*, 30th anniversary ed. Center City: Hazelden Publishing, 2024.

Cregg, David R. and Jennifer S. Cheavens. "Gratitude Interventions: Effective Self-Help? A Meta-Analysis of the Impact on Symptoms of Depression and Anxiety." *Journal of Happiness Studies* 22 (2021): 413–45. https://doi.org/10.1007/s10902-020-00236-6.

Crossan, Mary M., Alyson Byrne, Gerard H. Seijts, Mark Reno, Lucas Monzani, and Jeffrey Gandz. "Toward a Framework of Leader Character in Organizations." *Journal of Management Studies* 57, no. 1 (November 2017): 986–1018.

Cuddy, Amy. "Your Body Language May Shape Who You Are." October 1, 2012. https://www.youtube.com/watch?v=Ks-_Mh1QhMc&t=647s.

DePaul, Kristi. "What Does It Really Take to Build a New Habit?" *Harvard Business Review*, February 2, 2021. https://hbr.org/2021/02/what-does-it-really-take-to-build-a-new-habit.

DeSteno, David. *Emotional Success*. New York: HarperCollins, 2019.

Duke, Annie. *Quit: The Power of Knowing When to Walk Away*. New York: Portfolio, 2020.

Dutton Jane E., Kristina M. Workman, and Ashley Hardin. "Compassion at Work." *Annual Review of Organizational Psychology and Organizational Behavior* 1, no. 1 (March 2014): 277–304.

Elsesser, Kim. "The Debate on Power Posing Continues: Here's Where We Stand," *Forbes*, October 2, 2020. https://www.forbes.com/sites/kimelsesser/2020/10/02/the-debate-on-power-posing-continues-heres-where-we-stand.

Elving, Wim J. L., "The Role of Communication in Organisational Change." *Corporate Communications: An International Journal* 10, no. 2 (June 2005):129–38. http://doi.org/10.1108/13563280510596943.

Emmons, Robert A. "Gratitude: Greatest of the Virtues or the Undignified Badge of Surrender? Myths and Realities." (Beimfohr-Neuss Distinguished Lecture, Chesterton House, Cornell University, Ithaca, NY, and Zoom, November 3, 2022).

Eurich, Tasha. "What Self-Awareness Really Is (and How to Cultivate It)," *Harvard Business Review*, January 4, 2018, https://hbr.org/2018/01/what-self-awareness-really-is-and-how-to-cultivate-it.

Frankl, Viktor E. *Man's Search for Meaning*. New York: Pocket Books, 1959.

French, Sandra L. and Tracey Quigley Holden. "Positive Organizational Behavior: A Buffer for Bad News." *Business Communication Quarterly* 75, no 4 (June 2012): 208–20. https://doi.org/10.1177/1080569912441823.

Friedman, Maurice. *Encounter on the Narrow Ridge: A Life of Martin Burber*. New York: Paragon House, 1991.

Gaba, Sherry. "All-or-Nothing Thinking in Addiction." *Psychology Today*, June 25, 2019. https://www.psychologytoday.com/us/blog/addiction-and-recovery/ 201906/all-or-nothing-thinking-in-addiction.

Holiday, Ryan and Stephen Hanselman. *Lives of the Stoics: The Art of Living from Zeno to Marcus Aurelius.* New York: Portfolio/Penguin, 2002.

Kraut, Richard. "Aristotle's Ethics." *The Stanford Encyclopedia of Philosophy*, eds. Edward N. Zalta and Uri Nodelman. July 2, 2022. https://plato.stanford. edu/archives/fall2022/entries/aristotle-ethics.

Goetz, Jennifer L., Dacher Keltner, and Emiliana Simon-Thomas. "Compassion: An Evolutionary Analysis and Empirical Review." *Psychological Bulletin* 136, no. 3 (May 2010): 351–74.

Gragnano, Andrea, Silvia Simbula, and Massimo Miglioretti. "Work-Life Balance: Weighing the Importance of Work-Family and Work-Health Balance." *International Journal of Environmental Research and Public Health* 17, no. 3 (2020).

Grant, Adam. *Give and Take: Why Helping Others Drives Our Success.* London: Penguin Publishing Group, 2014.

Griffin, Kevin. *One Breath at a Time: Buddhism and the Twelve Steps.* St. Martin's Press, 2004.

Hamilton. "Non-Stop" Lyrics. Accessed March 7, 2024. https://www.azlyrics. com/lyrics/linmanuelmiranda/nonstop.html.

Harari, Dana, Brian W. Swider, Laurens Bujold Steed, and Amy P. Breidenthal. "Is Perfect Good? A Meta-Analysis of Perfectionism in the Workplace." *Journal of Applied Psychology* 103, no. 10 (2018): 1121–44. http://doi.org/10.1037/ apl0000324.

Hautala, Laura. "Amazon Adjusts 'Time Off Task' Policy that Critics Said Limited Bathroom Breaks." *CNET*, June 2, 2021. https://www.cnet.com/ tech/tech-industry/amazon-adjusts-time-off-task-policy-that-critics-said -limited-bathroom-breaks.

Hazelden Betty Ford Foundation. "Boundaries in Addiction Recovery." August 24, 2018. https://www.hazeldenbettyford.org/articles/boundaries-in -addiction-recovery.

Hirschman, Albert O. *Exit, Voice, and Loyalty: Responses to Decline in Firms, Organizations, and States.* Cambridge, Harvard University Press, 1970.

Ibarra, Herminia. "The Authenticity Paradox: Why Feeling Like a Fake Can Be a Sign of Growth." *Harvard Business Review*, January 2015. http:// www.contracostalocalgovtacademy.com/uploads/3/8/1/3/38138031/hbr --authenticity_paradox.pdf.

Intel. "Powerless to Purpose: Dr. Brandon Marin Shares His Story to Inspire Change." We Are Intel. December 15, 2021. https://community.intel. com/t5/Blogs/Intel/We-Are-Intel/From-Powerless-to-Purpose-Dr-Brandon -Marin-Shares-His-Story-to/post/1344036.

Jans-Beken, Lilian, Nele Jacobs, Mayke Janssens, Sanne Peeters, Jennifer Reijnders, Lilian Lechner, and Johan Lataster. "Gratitude and Health: An Updated Review." *The Journal of Positive Psychology* 15, no. 6 (November 2020): 1-40. https://doi.org/10.1080/17439760.2019.1651888.

Ji, Hyunjoo. "Blowing the Whistle in South Korea: Hyundai Man Takes on Chaebol Culture." Reuters. May 15, 2017. https://www.reuters.com/article/us-hyundai-whistleblower-idUSKCN18B0J5.

Kanter, Rosabeth Moss. "Managing Yourself." *Harvard Business Review*, March 2011. https://hbr.org/2011/03/managingyourself-zoom-in-zoom-out.

Kidder, Rushworth M. *Moral Courage*. New York: HarperCollins, 2005.

Kitroeff, Natalie, David Gelles, and Jack Nicas. "Boeing 737 Max Safety System Was Vetoed, Engineer Says." *The New York Times,* October 2, 2019. https://www.nytimes.com/2019/10/02/business/boeing-737-max-crashes.html.

Knight, Rebecca. "How to Manage Your Perfectionism." *Harvard Business Review*, April 29, 2019. https://hbr.org/2019/04/how-to-manage-your-perfectionism.

Kross, Ethan. *Chatter: The Voice in Our Head, Why It Matters, and How to Harness It.* New York: Crown, 2021.

Kumar, Amit and Nicholas Epley. "Undervaluing Gratitude: Expressers Misunderstand the Consequences of Showing Appreciation." *Psychological Science* 29, no. 9 (June 2018): 1423–35.

Lamott, Anne. *Help, Thanks, Wow: The Three Essential Prayers*. Riverhead Books, 2012.

Leary, Mark R., Kate J. Diebels, Erin K. Davisson, Katrina P. Jongman-Sereno, Jennifer C. Isherwood. "Cognitive and Interpersonal Features of Intellectual Humility." *Personality and Social Psychology Bulletin* 43, no. 6 (March 2017): 793–813.

Levine, Emma E. and Maurice E. Schweitzer. "Are Liars Ethical? On the Tension Between Benevolence and Honesty." *Journal of Experimental Social Psychology* 53, no. 3 (July 2014): 108.

Lewis, C.S. "The Screwtape Letters." *The Guardian*, May 2, 1941. Samizdat Ebooks, 2016. https://www.samizdat.qc.ca/arts/lit/PDFs/ScrewtapeLetters_CSL.pdf, 63.

Lieberman, Charlotte. "Why You Procrastinate (It Has Nothing to Do With Self-Control)." *The New York Times*, March 25, 2019. https://www.nytimes.com/2019/03/25/smarter-living/why-you-procrastinate-it-has-nothing-to-do-with-self-control.html.

Lopez, Shane. "The Science of Hope: An Interview with Shane Lopez," Earl E. Bakken Center for Spirituality & Healing. Accessed December 11, 2023. The University of Minnesota, https://www.takingcharge.csh.umn.edu/science-hope-interview-shane-lopez.

Lv, Jing, Yuanchen Jiang, Runze Li, Yanyan Chen, Xiaodan Gu, Jingyi Zhou, Yuan Zheng, et al. "Effects of Loving-Kindness and Compassion Meditations on Self-Compassion: A Systematic Review and Meta-Analysis." *Clinical Psychology-Science and Practice* (September 2023): 1–18, http://doi.org/10.1037/cps0000177.

Marijuana Anonymous World Services. *Life with Hope: A Return to Living Through the 12 Steps and the 12 Traditions of Marijuana Anonymous*, 3rd ed. Walnut: A New Leaf Publications, 2017.

Mashal, Nehjla M. Sherry A. Beaudreau, Michael A. Hernandez, Rachel Cackler Duller, Holly Romaniak, Ki Eun Shin, Ken A. Paller, and Richard E. Zinbarg. "A Brief Worry Reappraisal Paradigm (REAP) Increases Coping with Worries." *Cognitive Therapy and Research* 44 (November 2019): 216–28. https://doi.org/10.1007/s10608-019-10053-8.

Mayo, Charles. Quoted in Leonard Louis Levinson. *Bartlett's Unfamiliar Quotations*. Chicago: Cowles Book Company, Inc., 1971.

McGregor, Jena. "Maya Angelou on Leadership, Courage and the Creative Process." *The Washington Post*, May 28, 2014. www.washingtonpost.com/news/on-leadership/wp/2014/05/28/maya-angelou-on-leadership-courage-and-the-creative-process.

Molinsky, Andy. "If You're Not Outside Your Comfort Zone, You Won't Learn Anything," *Harvard Business Review*, July 29, 2016. https://hbr.org/2016/07/if-youre-not-outside-your-comfort-zone-you-wont-learn-anything.

Nakken, Craig, *Finding Your Moral Compass: Transformative Principles to Guide You in Recovery and Life*. Hazelden Publishing, 2011.

Narcotics Anonymous. "Just for Today." Accessed March 17, 2024, https://jftna.org/jft.

Neff, Kristin D. "Self-Compassion Guided Practices and Exercises." Accessed January 17, 2024. https://self-compassion.org/category/exercises/#exercises.

Nelson, Noelle, Selin Malkoc, and Baba Shiv. "Emotions Know Best: The Advantage of Emotional Versus Cognitive Responses to Failure." *Journal of Behavioral Decision Making* 31, no. 1 (2018): 40–51, https://doi.org/10.1002/bdm.2042.

Newman, Amy, *Business Communication and Character*, 11th ed. Boston: Cengage, 2023.

———. "How to Feel Confident for a Presentation and Manage Speech Anxiety." Accessed December 21, 2023. https://speaking.amynewman.com/speakingapp.php.

———. "Motivations and Risks of Demonstrating Courage." eCornell. Online course. *Courage, Humility, and Compassion*. Accessed March 14, 2024.

———. "Preparing for Difficult Conversations." eCornell. Online course. *Courage, Humility, and Compassion*. Accessed February 25, 2024.

P., Bill, Todd W., and Sara S. *Drop the Rock*, 2ⁿᵈ ed. Seattle: Hazelden Publishing, 2005.

Palmer, Alan H. "Stop Asking 'Why' and Start Asking 'How.'" *Harvard Business Review*, October 18, 2021. https://hbr.org/2021/10/stop-asking-why-and -start-asking-how.

Peterson, Christopher and Martin Seligman. *Character Strengths and Virtues: A Handbook and Classification*. Washington: American Psychological Association / Oxford University Press, 2004.

Pink, Daniel H. *Drive: The Surprising Truth About What Motivates Us*. New York: Riverhead Books, 2009.

Pittman, Bill. *Practice These Principles and What Is the Oxford Group?* Center City: Hazelden, 1997; rev. from *What Is the Oxford Group*, 1933.

Plante, Joseph M. J. "The Role of Personal Hope in Career Advancement." Indiana Wesleyan University. ProQuest Dissertations Publishing (2021). https://www. proquest.com/openview/cf76f0ebe1fc8d29ac69b57217dcf2d6/1: 1–135.

Pommier, Elizabeth, Kristin D. Neff, and István Tóth-Király. "The Development and Validation of the Compassion Scale." *Assessment* 27, no. 4 (April 2019): 21–39. https://doi.org/10.1177/1073191119874108.

Raes, Filip, Elizabeth Pommier, Kristin D. Neff, and Dinska Van Gucht. "Construction and Factorial Validation of a Short Form of the Self -Compassion Scale." *Clinical Psychology and Psychotherapy* 18, no. 3 (May– June 2011): 250–55.

Rasmussen, Kyler R., Madelynn Stackhouse, Susan D. Boon, Karly Comstock, and Rachel Ross. "Meta-Analytic Connections between Forgiveness and Health: The Moderating Effects of Forgiveness-Related Distinctions." *Psychology and Health* 34, no. 5 (2019): 515–34, http://doi.org/10.1080/08 870446.2018.1545906.

Reisinger, Holger and Dane Fetterer. "Forget Flexibility: Your Employees Want Autonomy." *Harvard Business Review*, October 29, 2021. https://hbr. org/2021/10/forget-flexibility-your-employees-want-autonomy.

Robbins, Mel. "The 'Let Them Theory.'" *The Mel Robbins Podcast*. Episode 70, May 2023. https://www.melrobbins.com/podcasts/episode-70.

Sahi, Razia S., Zhouzhou He, Jennifer A Silvers, and Naomi I Eisenberger. "One Size Does Not Fit All: Decomposing the Implementation and Differential Benefits of Social Emotion Regulation Strategies." *Emotion* 23, no 6 (September 2023): 1522–35. http://doi.org/10.1037/emo0001194.

Samuel, Sigal. "Why Cornel West Is Hopeful (But Not Optimistic)." Vox. July 20, 2020. https://www.vox.com/future-perfect/2020/7/29/21340730/ cornel-west-coronavirus-racism-way-through-podcast.

Sawyer, Katrina B., Christian N. Thoroughgood, Elizabeth E. Stillwell, Michelle K. Duffy, Kristin L. Scott, Elizabeth A. Adair. "Being Present and Thankful: A

Multi-Study Investigation of Mindfulness, Gratitude, and Employee Helping Behavior." *Journal of Applied Psychology* 107, no. 2 (2022): 240–62. https://doi.org/10.1037/apl0000903.

Schulz, Charles M. *Peanuts*, October 19, 1972. Retrieved from Fandom. https://peanuts.fandom.com/wiki/October_1972_comic_strips.

Schumann, Karina and Anna Dragotta. "Empathy as a Predictor of High-Quality Interpersonal Apologies." *European Journal of Social Psychology* 51, no. 6 (October 2021): 896–909.

Schumann, Karina. "An Affirmed Self and a Better Apology: The Effect of Self-Affirmation on Transgressors' Responses to Victims, *Journal of Experimental Social Psychology* 54 (September 2014): 89–96.

Schwarz, Roger. "The 'Sandwich Approach' Undermines Your Feedback." *Harvard Business Review*, April 19, 2003. https://hbr.org/2013/04/the-sandwich-approach-undermin.

Scioli, Anthony, Michael Ricci, Than Nyugen, and Erica Scioli. "Hope: Its Nature and Measurement." *Psychology of Religion and Spirituality* 3, no. 2 (May 2011): 78–97. http://doi.org/10.1037/a0020903.

Scott, Kim. *Radical Candor: Be a Kick-Ass Boss Without Losing Your Humanity.* New York: St. Martin's Press, 2017.

Seijts, Gerard, Mary Crossan, and Erica Carleton. "Embedding Leader Character into HR Practices to Achieve Sustained Excellence." *Organizational Dynamics* 46, no. 1 (February 2017): 30–39.

Shanahan, Lilly, Sherika Hill, Lauren Gaydosh, Annekatrin Steinhoff, Elizabeth Costello, Kenneth Dodge, Kathleen Harris, William Copeland. "Does Despair Really Kill? A Roadmap for an Evidence-Based Answer." *American Journal of Public Health* 109, no. 6 (June 2019): 854–58. http://doi.org/10.2105/AJPH.2019.305016.

Shonk, Katie, "3 Types of Conflict and How to Address Them." Harvard Law School Program on Negotiation. October 1, 2020. www.pon.harvard.edu/daily/conflict-resolution/types-conflict.

SHRM. "What Should an Employer Tell a Candidate Who Is Not Selected for the Position?" Accessed March 4, 2024. www.shrm.org/ResourcesAndTools/tools-and-samples/hr-qa/Pages/whatshouldanemployertellarejectedcandidate.aspx.

Simons, Tony. *The Integrity Dividend: Leading by the Power of Your Word.* San Francisco: Jossey-Bass, 2008.

Singer, Tania and Olga M. Klimecki. "Empathy and Compassion. *Current Biology* 24, no. 18 (2014).

Slemp, Gavin R., Margaret L. Kern, Kent J. Patrick, and Richard M. Ryan, "Leader Autonomy Support in the Workplace: A Meta-Analytic Review." *Motivation and Emotion* 42 (May 2018): 706–24. https://doi.org/10.1007/s11031-018-9698-y.

Snyder, Charles R. "Hope Theory: Rainbows in the Mind." *Psychological Inquiry* 13, no. 4 (October 2002): 249–75, http://doi.org/10.1207/S15327965PLI1304_01F.

Southwick, Daniel A., Chia-Jung Tsay, and Angela L. Duckworth. "Grit at Work." *Research in Organizational Behavior* 39 (2021): 100126. https://doi.org/10.1016/j.riob.2020.100126.

Steller, Jennifer E., Vida M. Manzo, Michael W. Kraus, and Dacher Keltner. "Class and Compassion: Socioeconomic Factors Predict Responses to Suffering." *Emotion* 12, no. 3 (December 2011): 449–59.

Taitz, Jenny. "Honest Communication in the Age of Ghosting." *The Wall Street Journal*, August 21, 2021. https://www.wsj.com/articles/honest-communication-in-the-age-of-ghosting-11630070801.

Taub, Rabbi Shais. *God of Our Understanding: Jewish Spirituality and Recovery from Addiction*. Jersey City: KTAV Publishing House, 2011.

Tessema, Mussie T., Kathryn J. Ready, and Abel B. Embaye, "The Effects of Employee Recognition, Pay, and Benefits on Job Satisfaction: Cross Country Evidence." *Journal of Business and Economics* 4, no.1 (2013): 1–12.

Troup, Calvin L. and Christina L. McDowell Marinchak, "Niceness, Flattery, and Deceit." *Western Journal of Communication* 82, no. 1 (January–February 2018): 59–74, http://doi.org/10.1080/10570314.2017.1306097.

Ulanov, Ann and Barry Ulanov. *Primary Speech: A Psychology of Prayer*. Atlanta: John Knox Press, 1982.

University of Notre Dame. Science of Generosity. "What Is Generosity?" Accessed February 29, 2024. https://generosityresearch.nd.edu/more-about-the-initiative/what-is-generosity.

Uysal, H. Tezcan and Fatma Yilmaz. "Procrastination in the Workplace: The Role of Hierarchical Career Plateau." *Upravlenets – The Manager* 11, no. 3 (June 2020): 82–101. http://doi.org/10.29141/2218-5003-2020-11-3-7.

Vakola, Maria. "The Reasons Behind Change Recipients' Behavioral Reactions: A Longitudinal Investigation." *Journal of Managerial Psychology* 31, no. 1 (February 2016): 202–15.

Van den Bosch, Ralph and Toon W. Taris. "Authenticity at Work: Development and Validation of an Individual Authenticity Measure at Work." *Journal of Happiness Studies* 15, no. 1 (February 2014): 1–18.

Van Gordon, William. "Why an Inferiority Complex Can Still Mean a Big Ego." *Psychology Today*, August 31, 2020. https://www.psychologytoday.com/us/blog/contemplative-psychology/202008/why-inferiority-complex-can-still-mean-big-ego.

W., Bill. to Dr. Carl Gustav Jung. Letter. January 23, 1961.

———. "The Next Frontier: Emotional Sobriety." *AA Grapevine*, January 1958. https://www.aagrapevine.org/magazine/1958/jan/next-frontier-emotional-sobriety.

———. *Twelve Steps and Twelve Traditions*, 75ᵗʰ printing. New York: Alcoholics Anonymous World Services, Inc., 2011.

Walker, Val. *The Art of Comforting*. London: Penguin, 2010.

Warren, Rick. *The Purpose Driven Life: What on Earth Am I Here For?* (Grand Rapids: Zondervan, 2012).

Watts, Richard E., and Jerry Trusty. "Using Imaginary Team Members in Reflecting 'As If.'" *Journal of Constructivist Psychology* 16, no. 4 (October 2003): 335–40. http://doi.org/10.1080/10720530390227676.

White, Louis. "The Age of Entitlement: How to Manage Demanding Employees." *Human Resources Director*, April 11, 2022. https://www.hcamag.com/ca/specialization/employee-engagement/the-age-of-entitlement-how-to-manage-demanding-employees/402324.

Wood, Alex, Alex Linley, John Maltby, Michael Baliousis, and Joseph Stephen. "The Authentic Personality: A Theoretical and Empirical Conceptualization and the Development of the Authenticity Scale." *Journal of Counseling Psychology* 55, no. 3 (July 2008): 385–99.

Workaholics Anonymous. "The Twenty Questions." Accessed February 15, 2024. https://workaholics-anonymous.org/10-literature/24-twenty-questions.

Worline, Monica C. "Courage in Organizations: An Integrative Review of the 'Difficult Virtue.'" In *The Oxford Handbook of Positive Organizational Scholarship* edited by Gretchen M. Spreitzer and Kim S. Cameron. Oxford University Press, 2011.

Worline, Monica C. and Jane E. Dutton. *Awakening Compassion at Work*. Oakland: Berrett-Koehler, 2017.

About the Author

Amy Newman retired with emeritus status from teaching management communication at the Cornell SC Johnson College of Business. Before Cornell, Amy had a successful but unfulfilling career in corporate human resources. She is the author of *Business Communication and Character* (11th ed.), and *Building Leadership Character*. When she's not writing, Amy is hiking, kayaking, playing the drums, or at a recovery meeting.

Index

OTHER TITLES IN THE BUSINESS CAREER DEVELOPMENT COLLECTION

Vilma Barr, Consultant, Editor

- *Working in Business and Finance* by Joseph Malgesini
- *Make Your Internship Count* by Marti Fischer
- *Sales Excellence* by Eden White
- *How to Think Strategically* by Greg Githens
- *Succeeding as a Young Entrepreneur* by Harvey Morton
- *The Intentional Mindset* by Jane Frankel
- *Still Room for Humans* by Stan Schatt
- *Am I Doing This Right?* by Tony D. Thelen, Matthew C. Mitchell and Jeffrey A. Kappen
- *Telling Your Story, Building Your Brand* by Henry Wong
- *Social Media Is About People* by Cassandra Bailey and Dana M. Schmidt
- *Pay Attention!* by Cassandra M. Bailey and Dana M. Schmidt
- *Remaining Relevant* by Karen Lawson
- *The Road to Champagne* by Alejandro Colindres Frañó
- *Burn Ladders. Build Bridges* by Alan M. Patterson
- *Decoding Your STEM Career* by Peter J Devenyi
- *The Networking Playbook* by Darryl Howes

Concise and Applied Business Books

The Collection listed above is one of 30 business subject collections that Business Expert Press has grown to make BEP a premiere publisher of print and digital books. Our concise and applied books are for...

- Professionals and Practitioners
- Faculty who adopt our books for courses
- Librarians who know that BEP's Digital Libraries are a unique way to offer students ebooks to download, not restricted with any digital rights management
- Executive Training Course Leaders
- Business Seminar Organizers

Business Expert Press books are for anyone who needs to dig deeper on business ideas, goals, and solutions to everyday problems. Whether one print book, one ebook, or buying a digital library of 110 ebooks, we remain the affordable and smart way to be business smart. For more information, please visit www.businessexpertpress.com, or contact sales@businessexpertpress.com.